The Real World in Which We Live:

The Social Rules and Social System under Which We Suffer, Struggle, Survive and Prosper

The Real World in Which We Live:

The Social Rules and Social System under Which We Suffer, Struggle, Survive and Prosper

Manfred Davidmann

Social Organisation Limited

Published by Social Organisation Limited
Euro House, 1394 High Road, London, N20 9YZ, United Kingdom
Contact: books@socialorganisation.eu
www.socialorganisation.eu

Manfred Davidmann looks at what people are struggling against to find out why people have to struggle throughout their adult lives, in all countries and organisations, at all levels, to maintain and improve their standard of living and quality of life. He reviews and analyses ownership and deciding policy, multinational summits and agreements, top-level decision-making and democracy, exporting and importing of employment and unemployment, transfer pricing and taxation, how society is organised for controlling and exploiting people, taxing the population for private profit, corrupted economics and misguided (misleading) experts, creating, patenting and marketing of new forms of life, and more.

He describes and defines motivation and what people are struggling to achieve, and 'participation in decision-making'.

Published by Social Organisation Ltd in 2016

ISBN 978-0-85192-058-0

Printed and bound by Witley Press Ltd
24-26 Greevegate, Hunstantan, Norfolk, PE36 6AD, United Kingdom

Cover design by Dr. Angelika Schaumberg

CONTENTS

Multinational (Global) Operations

What People are Struggling Against

What People are Struggling to Achieve

The author Manfred Davidmann wrote and compiled this book's content from Chapter 2 to Chapter 18 and chose the book's title. Unfortunately he was not able to complete and finish his work on this book.

In accordance with Manfred Davidmann's will and wishes this book is now published. It contains the author's last manuscript (Chapter 2 to Chapter 18).

Following Manfred Davidmann's wording and style, the description on page 4, 'Contents', 'Overview' (Chapter 1) and the text for the cover's back page have been added in order to complete the book for publication.

Dr. Angelika Schaumberg, Social Organisation Limited, 2016

Overview

Ownership and Deciding Policy   (Chapters 2 to 6)

2   Ownership

Ownership means control, means decision-taking. This short review covers where the right to ownership comes from and how it is exercised. Ownership of land, means of production, and wealth. Ownership in relation to incomes, need, and human rights.

3   Ownership and Limited Liability

This report discusses different types of enterprises and the extent to which owners are responsible for repaying the debts of their enterprise.

Also discussed are disadvantages, difficulties and abuses associated with the system of Limited Liability, and their implications for customers, suppliers and employees.

4   Community and Public Ownership

This report is an objective evaluation of community ownership and reviews the reasons both for nationalising and for privatising.

Performance, management, control and accountability of community-owned enterprises and industries are discussed.

A number of striking case-studies clearly illustrate the points being made.

5   Ownership and Deciding Policy: Companies, Shareholders, Directors and Community

A short statement which describes the system by which a company's majority shareholders decide policy and control the company.

6   Multinational Summits and Agreements, Top-level Decision-making and Democracy

Describes how secretive top-level multinational meetings and trading agreements appear to be taking control over key aspects of the internal affairs of participating countries, taking control away from elected governments, giving the control to multinational corporations and top-level organisations.

Shows that publicity about what is being planned or taking place is an effective deterrent.

Multinational (Global) Operations   (Chapters 7 to 9)

7   Exporting and Importing of Employment and Unemployment

This report discusses both exporting and importing of employment and unemployment, the underlying principles and the effect of trade between low-wage and high-wage countries.

It shows what is required to halt and reverse the trend towards increasing unemployment and falling living standards in high-wage countries.

The report not only shows what is required to make the system work, but also the controls required to prevent misuse of the system and to protect people.

There are sections about transferring operations abroad, about importing from low-wage countries, about social costs of unemployment, about community objectives and community support for enterprises, about ownership rights and about ensuring that the behaviour of enterprises is socially responsible.

8   Transfer Pricing and Taxation

One of the most controversial and often least understood operations of multinationals, transfer pricing, is clearly described and defined.

An easily-followed illustration shows how transfer pricing can be used by multinationals to maximise their profits by tax avoidance and by obtaining tax rebates.

Also discussed is the effect of transfer pricing on the tax burden carried by other tax payers.

9   Creating, Patenting and Marketing of New Forms of Life

This report evaluates what is happening in genetic manipulation, and in the worldwide application and use of new life-forms by multinationals.

The moral and ethical questions raised are considerable, public health risks are high, and the report looks at trends from the point of view of the community.

Changed and new life-forms can now be owned by multinational corporations, generation after generation. The report evaluates what is happening to private ownership of life-forms as a result of the GATT agreement. It would seem that the nature of profit-orientated multinationals threatens public health, and that independence and freedom are at risk.

The report contains important far-reaching conclusions and recommendations about man-made forms of life, the food we eat, the direction in which multinationals are moving and their aims, how to control what is happening and how to improve the trend of events.

What People are Struggling Against   (Chapters 10 to 14)

10   What People are Struggling Against: How Society is Organised for Controlling and Exploiting People

This main report brings together key conclusions from the following four studies which were undertaken to find out and to obtain a better understanding of why people have to struggle throughout their adult lives, in all countries and organisations, at all levels, to maintain and improve their standard of living and quality of life. We know what people are struggling to achieve and so this study was undertaken to explore why people have to struggle by looking at what they are struggling against.

11   Democracy Under Attack: Top-level Leadership and Decision-making

Discusses and illustrates the internal struggles taking place in companies (corporations), political parties and all other organisations, for achieving greater democracy and against those wishing to overpower democratic processes of decision-taking.

Describes participative organisation (democracy), the basic criteria by which it can be judged and the processes by which leaderships attempt to take over the decision-taking processes.

12   Understanding How Society is Organised for Controlling and Exploiting People

Describes the various ways in which corporations (companies) accumulate their capital and reserves from moneys taken from customers. Enterprises are allowed to collect, take over and control such moneys and co-operatives also take over moneys from their members.

The report looks at ownership, at the right to own property, and at the way society and our activities are organised and controlled to enable possessions and wealth to be accumulated by a few people at the expense of the population.

13   Taxing the Population for Private Profit

This report shows how taxpayers' moneys are used in different ways to enlarge the profits of companies (corporations) and thus of their owners. Companies (corporations) are in effect allowed to tax the population and are also allowed to pass large parts of their operating costs to the taxpayers.

Moneys saved by spending less on social security for those in need and gained by collecting more tax from the working population, is apparently being used to reduce the taxes collected from the rich and from corporations.

14   Corrupted Economics and Misguided (Misleading) Experts

This report shows how 'Economics' is used to misinform and mislead the general public, and looks at the role and vested interests of experts.

So this report discusses the relevance and reliability of some economic relationships, clearly stating them and the underlying considerations as well as commenting on misleading political interpretations and misuses of the work of economists.

Subjects discussed include the cost of living, the fight against inflation, index linking, unemployment, uses of the base interest rate, share prices, currency exchange rates, the role and vested interests of experts.

What People are Struggling to Achieve   (Chapters 15 to 17)

15   Using Words to Communicate Effectively

Shows how to communicate more effectively, covering aspects of thinking, writing, speaking and listening as well as formal and informal communications.

Consists of guidelines found useful by university students and practising middle and senior managers.

16 The Will to Work: What People Struggle to Achieve

In this major review, analysis and report Manfred Davidmann clearly defines and describes motivation, its basis and 'motivating'.

Starting by considering motivation from the point of view of the employer (productivity, remuneration, job satisfaction), this leads to considering what people want and what they struggle to achieve.

A key part of the report is community orientated, including a detailed step-by-step listing of what people are struggling to achieve, their needs and wants, their achievements and objectives. This progression shows underdeveloped and developed people as they are, human beings at different stages of an identical struggle for a better life against those who wish to profit from their condition.

And you can assess how far the country/community you are living in has advanced in this struggle for independence and a good life for all, or where you are yourself on this scale.

Highlights are Figure 1 (Motivation of Directors) and Figure 3 (People's Needs and Wants, Achievements and Objectives: The Struggle for Independence and a Good Life).

17 Quotable Quotes about Democracy in the Real World

The Meaning of Democracy
The Right to Education
The Right to Decide
The Right to Strike
Role of Experts

Selecting and Electing Representatives
    Proportional Representation: 'Closed-list' and 'Open-list' Systems
    Closed-list System
    UK Members of European Parliament (MEPs)
    Proportional Representation in Israel

Top-level Decision-taking and Democracy
Multinational Summits and Agreements

The Right to Know
    Open Decision-taking (in Government, Enterprises, Organisations)
    Access to Information
    Whistle-blowing

Ownership

Ownership

What you see here has to a considerable extent been drawn from two previously-published works by Manfred Davidmann {1, 2}, bringing together in one place material from these and a number of earlier reports.

Ownership is the right to possess something and to decide what is to be done with it. If I own something it belongs to me and I decide what to do with it. An example would be owning a house.

Possession is having something in one's custody as distinct from owning it. If I possess something it belongs to another but I can decide how to use it. An example would be renting a house.

Another example is deciding what to do with one's money (ownership) or deciding on and controlling the use of money belonging to someone else (possession).

Regarding the right to ownership, two questions need to be considered, namely: where does the right come from and how is it exercised?

Rights to own property differ from one society to another. Ownership rights are based on man-made laws and there has been little, if any, grass-roots community-orientated participation in their drafting. Ownership laws which assign ownership 'rights' have been devised by the owners themselves or by those who serve them.

Private ownership of land and means of production, of funds and wealth, has always been accumulated at someone else's expense. Originally all belonged to the community, belonged to all alike.

A human right is something one may legally or morally claim, is the state of being entitled to a privilege or immunity or authority to act. Human rights are those held to be claimable by any living person, apply to all living people. Every living person is entitled to them.

So ownership of land and means of production, of funds and wealth, rightfully belongs to the community, belongs to all alike, is a human right. Those who have accumulated ownership rights have only possession, which means they can use and apply ownership rights but may do so only on behalf of, and for the benefit of, the community and that they are accountable to the community for the way in which they do so.

Hence we have the use of possessions as long as we use them to provide a good living for our family, and beyond that for the benefit of the community, of others less able or fortunate. For the benefit of the community around us and then for the benefit of communities abroad.

But we may only support those who themselves genuinely support our benevolent ideals and principles and their application and who themselves live and act accordingly, who behave humanely.

Ownership means control, means deciding policy. And democratic deciding of policy, that is democratic control, ensures that it is producers, customers and the community as a whole who benefit.

Whoever takes policy decisions, deciding what has to be done and what is to be achieved, controls. It is grass-roots producers, customers and community members who must take policy decisions, who must decide what has to be done and what has to be achieved.

What is at stake is ownership of the means of production, of an independent source of income. Also at stake is freedom from exploitation and from oppression through need.

References

{1} See chapter 5,
'Ownership and Deciding Policy: Companies,
Shareholders, Directors and Community'
Manfred Davidmann

{2} 'Cooperatives and Cooperation:
Causes of Failure, Guidelines for Success'
Manfred Davidmann
ISBN 978-0-85192-056-6

Chapter 3

Ownership and Limited Liability

Summary

This report discusses different types of enterprises and the extent to which owners are responsible for repaying the debts of their enterprise.

Also discussed are disadvantages, difficulties and abuses associated with the system of Limited Liability, and their implications for customers, suppliers and employees.

Ownership and Enterprises

It is customary to consider the different types of enterprises by ranking them by what appears to be according to size.

The usual list then consists of
    Sole Trader
    Partnership
    Private Company
    Public Company.

Considering them in the way they are defined in the UK, then a sole trader works on his own account. A partnership generally consists of up to twenty partners. The Private Company can have up to fifty owners (members) and its shares are not available to the general public. The Public Company, however, can have an unlimited number of owners

25

(shareholders) and its shares are quoted on the stock exchange and are available to the general public.

Public companies tend to have bigger sales than Private companies which in turn tend to be bigger than Partnerships which themselves tend to be bigger than Sole Traders. However, some Partnerships and some Private companies are very big indeed.

But ranking types of enterprises in this way misses really relevant distinctions between different types of enterprises. And one important characteristic which distinguishes one kind of enterprise from another is whether the owners benefit from 'Limited Liability'. <1>

Limited Liability

Fully Liable for Debts
(Having to pay back all one's debts)

People have to pay their debts, that is they are liable for the repayment of their debts to the full extent of their means, of their assets. All that one has, such as savings, investments, furniture, car and home, may have to be sold to pay one's debts.

In the same way a Sole Trader is fully liable for the debts of his enterprise. Similarly the partners in a Partnership are jointly fully liable for the repayment of the debts of their partnership.

Their possessions may have to be sold to pay the debts of their enterprises, that is to pay their debts.

But the owners of such enterprises do not need to publish their accounts and may be able to evade payment of debts by transferring possessions to relatives or by possibly removing them from the country's jurisdiction.

Limited Liability for Debts
(Of one's debts, having to pay back no more than a specified sum which can be much smaller than the debts)

What owners of Private and of Public companies have in common is that the liability of the owners for the debts of their companies is limited. Their liability is limited to the paid-up value of the shares they own and this means that it is limited to the amount they agreed to pay for the shares when they bought them.

When a company becomes insolvent, which means when the company cannot pay its debts, then it ceases to trade because it cannot pay its way. It is liquidated, that is its assets are sold and the resulting moneys used to pay at least some of its debts. The remainder, if any, is paid to its owners.

When companies become insolvent and cease to trade, they often owe enormous sums which they cannot repay. But the owner's liability is strictly limited by law to the amount he agreed to pay for the shares when he bought them. The owner is protected by law, his personal possessions cannot be used to repay the company's debts.

So there is now a much greater risk for those dealing with such enterprises if the enterprise becomes insolvent. The owners have transferred much if not most of the risk to suppliers (creditors), customers and employees. <2>

Suppliers may not get paid, customers can lose their down payments (deposits), customers can be left with worthless guarantees, employees may not be paid for work done, other moneys owed by the enterprise may not be repaid. The amounts involved may vastly exceed the enterprise's capital, the risk to suppliers and customers is often great, suppliers and customers lose very large sums each year.

Hence such enterprises generally have to indicate to those who have dealings with them that the enterprises' owners have passed much of the risk to suppliers and customers, that those dealing with the enterprise may not be repaid if it ceases to trade.

In the UK, for example, the law requires a company's name to include specified words, or their specified abbreviations, which in effect state the type of company and that suppliers and customers may lose their moneys if they have dealings with this company. A private company's name has to end with the word 'Limited' or the abbreviation 'Ltd'. A public company's name has to end with the word 'Company' or the abbreviation 'Co'. <3>

In Germany, the letters GmbH are used, for 'Gesellschaft mit beschraenkter Haftung', that is for a 'company with limited liability'. 'Inc' denotes a limited liability company in the United States.

It is because there is risk involved when dealing with companies that, in the UK, the larger companies also have to file each year independently audited summary accounts, as well as information about their directors, with the Registrar of Companies (and now with Companies House).

This information in this way becomes available to all who wish to check a company's creditworthiness, performance and progress.

But it takes time and money to obtain such information and knowledge and experience to understand, interpret and analyse the published information.

Owners take the profits but have transferred much of their risk to other people, to suppliers, customers and employees.

This benefits the owners but runs counter to the free-enterprise maxim that owners (capitalists) can earn profits by taking risks with their own money.

What we see is a system where owners enrich themselves by using and risking other people's moneys.

Customers Losing Out

Some companies are now so large and so many people have been affected at once that companies have been compelled by public pressure to make arrangements for compensating those losing out. Their trade associations have created funds for compensating customers for losses incurred as a result of a trader's insolvency. These funds are formed and replenished by collecting contributions from the trade association's member companies.

Trade associations hold funds which are then paid out to angry customers. The funds are collected from their member companies. The member companies recover the extra cost from their customers by increased prices.

Once again we see that owners have passed their risk to others, have in this way merely spread the losses among all their customers, are getting their customers as a whole to pay outstanding debts of insolvency.

Misuse by Owners and Directors

A company may be registered (incorporated), start trading, become insolvent and cease to trade after having incurred considerable debts which it cannot repay.

The owners and directors of that insolvent company may then at small cost register another company under a new name and continue trading under the new name, with similar results and more losses to the public.

While directors may be prohibited from holding office in certain circumstances, it would seem that such provisions do not at present effectively protect customers, suppliers and employees.

Role of Auditors

The audit is carried out by an independent person or partnership having approved qualifications. Their key role seems to be to ensure that an enterprise's annual summary accounts present a true and fair view of the financial outcome of the company's operations and of its assets, primarily for shareholders.

The appointment of auditors is generally approved by shareholders at the company's annual general meeting and auditors' fees are paid by the company. Which means that auditors may be selected and payment of their fees authorised by executive directors.

It is executive directors who are responsible for day-to-day operations and who are in the end accountable, to the shareholders, for the results obtained by the company.

And some directors may prefer to present their shareholders, suppliers and customers with a more favourable view of the company's situation than is warranted by actual results.

So the role of independent auditors would seem to be a difficult one.

Conclusions

1. Owners take the profits but have transferred much of their risk to other people, to suppliers, customers and employees.

    What we see is a system where owners enrich themselves by using and risking other people's moneys.

    This benefits the owners but runs counter to the free-enterprise maxim that owners may earn profits from taking risks with their own money.

2. While directors may be prohibited from holding office in certain circumstances, it would seem that such provisions do not at present effectively protect customers, suppliers and employees.

3. This is not really an acceptable situation.

Notes

<1> Enterprises whose owners have limited liability are called companies in the United Kingdom and corporations in the United States.

<2> Suppliers provide goods and services on credit, which means they get paid some time after the date on which the goods or services were provided, say two months later. If the company which is their customer becomes insolvent and ceases to trade, the supplier will not get paid for the goods and services he has already provided. He may be lucky and receive a part of the money owed to him but on the whole it is the supplier whose money is at risk and who loses out if the company becomes insolvent. Hence risk has been transferred by owners (shareholders) to suppliers.

Customers make advance payments to secure goods and services. If the company ceases to trade before these goods or services are provided, the customer is likely to lose all of his deposit. Similarly guarantees for goods bought or services provided are likely to be worthless if the company ceases to trade before the guarantee expires. The amount lost by customers at the present time in such ways in the UK is apparently of the order of £18 million each year.

Employees also lose out if a company becomes insolvent. Salaries, wages, holiday entitlement and redundancy compensation can be lost, quite apart from the social costs of the resulting unemployment to employees and to the community.

Banks also lose out when companies become insolvent. But banks are regarded as having much expertise in assessing the risks they take when lending money to their customers including companies. Assessing such risks is their business and they are paid for the risks they take by the interest paid to them for the loans they make.

<3> Recently changed so that a private company's name now ends with the words 'Company Limited' or the abbreviation 'Co Ltd'. A public company's name now ends with the words 'Public Limited Company' or the abbreviation 'PLC'.

Chapter 4

Community and Public Ownership

Summary

This report is an objective evaluation of community ownership and reviews the reasons both for nationalising and for privatising.

Performance, management, control and accountability of community-owned enterprises and industries are discussed.

A number of striking case-studies clearly illustrate the points being made.

Community and Public Ownership

We are here considering enterprises and industries which belong to, and are controlled by, the community.

Some of these are very big. The National Health Service in the UK, for example, was at one point the largest employer in the country, employing something like one million people.

The term 'nationalising' refers to the process of taking enterprises and industries into community ownership, 'privatising' refers to the process of returning them to private ownership.

'Community ownership' has elsewhere been called 'public ownership' and also 'common ownership'. But 'community ownership' is used here to get away from preconceived ideas and political propaganda which have become associated with the other terms.

Enterprises or industries in community ownership are often given labels such as National Corporation, Nationalised Industry, Public Corporation or Public Enterprise.

Such enterprises, however, trade just like privately owned enterprises and are often of comparable size to multinational corporations. What community-owned enterprises have in common is that they aim to serve the community.

Community-owned enterprises use surplus funds in the usual way for capital expenditure (new plant or equipment, updating or expanding) or repaying loans. And instead of paying dividends to private shareholders, remaining funds are passed to the government and so reduce the level of taxation. There are many ways in which surplus funds can be allocated between these categories.

When a community-owned enterprise requires financial support, the core consideration should be present and future service to the community, with the community providing required funds via the government.

Community owned enterprises were nationalised, that is taken into community ownership, for reasons connected with serving and protecting the community. They are accountable to the community for what they do and how they do it.

Important issues are

1. Aims and objectives,

2. Who appoints directors and chief executives and how they are appointed.

3. Accountability to the community of the enterprise, of its directors and chief executives, of those who appointed them and defined their aims and objectives.

Aims and Objectives

The first act of nationalisation in the UK was by a Conservative Government which nationalised the electricity grid in 1926 so as to rationalise and organise the supply of electricity.

The next act of nationalisation in the UK was carried out by a Labour Government which nationalised London's transport in 1933. Disorderly competition between private bus companies had been slowing down traffic and here also the need was to organise and improve a service to the community.

So the aims and objectives of community ownership, of nationalising enterprises or industries <1>, are as follows:

Aims

1. To provide an efficient and satisfactory level of service.

2. To ensure the supply of quality goods at reasonable prices.

3. To safeguard the community against exploitation.

Objectives

Included in the aims are these objectives:

1. To keep important and needed industries going which would collapse without government support.

2. To protect the community from being exploited by a monopoly, a monopoly being one which provides say 15 per cent or more of the total. The community must not be exploited when in need or when supplies are restricted. Profit mark-ups have to be reasonable in relation to actual costs incurred.

3. To provide capital when the amount to be invested or required is too big or when only a small or no return could be expected for a considerable time.

4. To provide and ensure essential public services in an effective way such as free education to the highest level, a national health service, public transport, postal service, energy and service utilities and public health.

Aims and objectives give priority to the community's needs and interests over purely profit making. For example, a loss-making industry may be kept going because national security requires this, or to prevent the rise in unemployment which might otherwise result.

But service to the community is not enough by itself. For the service to be effective there has also to be accountability to the community to ensure services and goods are being provided effectively.

Planning and Control of Activities and Performance

Planning and control of activities and performance are matters in which community-owned enterprises do not differ from other enterprises.

Consider Rolls-Royce.

The development of the RB211 aero-engine brought Rolls-Royce to insolvency in 1971 and it was nationalised by a conservative government to prevent its collapse.

About £500 million were invested in the company under public ownership by the community, as well as many hundreds of millions of pounds by way of research and development aid for new engine projects. In 1986 the government was providing about £150 million out of Rolls-Royce's £250 million spending on research and development and this level of government support was expected to continue after privatisation.

By 1987 Rolls-Royce had achieved a commercial market share of about 25 per cent for its engines, and it was returned to private ownership.

Here we see how an important industry was rescued from insolvency by nationalisation and later returned as a successful enterprise to private ownership.

However, one would like to see a factual analysis of the whole episode from cost of nationalising to final privatisation deal. Bearing in mind the considerable sums invested by the community in the company while it was nationalised, it seems that this acclaimed high-tech company was returned to private ownership at considerable loss to the community.

When there is no need to sell then it would seem that selling at a loss amounts to subsidising new owners.

An enterprise, however, is expected to make a profit after allowing for social costs and benefits, and this means that the enterprise's Profit and Loss Account has to include social costs and benefits. {2, 3}

Take the bitter struggle in 1985/86 in the UK between the Coal Board (which controlled the community-owned coal mining industry) and its workforce, the miners. The miners were defeated after about twelve months by top-level management which appeared to be following government policy.

The Coal Board apparently intended to close most coalmines while maintaining that commercial considerations (profitability) were the only criterion and that the Coal Board alone would decide which pits were to be closed, and when and how they were to be closed.

The miners opposed the unilateral closure of pits by the Coal Board, that is they opposed the closing of pits without first consulting its employees and the local community. In effect the miners maintained that the social benefits of keeping a mine going, and the social costs of closing a mine, to employees and to the local as well as to the national community, had to be taken into account.

Take REMPLOY, a company which has about 80 factories employing only disabled workers for producing a wide range of quality goods.

    1. Commercial considerations:
        (a) Unprofitable and making losses.
        (b) Subsidised by the community via the government of the day which makes up the losses.

    2. Social benefits:
        (a) Social security benefits saved which would otherwise have had to be paid by the government.
        (b) Income tax received by government from employees.

    3. Overall:
        Social benefits greater than the government's subsidy. In other words, a profitable operation from the point of view of the community as a whole.

    4. Add:
        Not quantified or included so far is the impact of paid employment on disabled employees who now see themselves as useful members of society doing needed and worth-while work.

In other words, the profitability of community-owned enterprises can only be assessed by including social benefits in Profit and Loss statements.

Community-owned industries are in effect monopolies and need independent, thorough and effective control of quality of service and pricing system. Much has been achieved in this area by government investigative committees.

Progress has also been made in controlling the pricing structures of national monopolies by government appointed committees with statutory powers to control prices and price systems.

However, what seems to be missing is effective public grassroots discussion, evaluation and participation in decision-making about basic policy matters. Such as the future of the industry, direction and speed of progress, quality of service and effectiveness of management.

Protecting the Community

British Oxygen Company, a privately owned British multinational, then sole supplier of oxygen in the UK, was investigated to determine whether they were using their monopoly power against the public interest. The inquiry found, for example, that uneconomic but essential supplies to small consumers, such as small garages and farmers, were being subsidised by large industrial tonnage-oxygen customers. British Oxygen was not misusing its monopoly power and was allowed to continue as before.

If the inquiry had found that British Oxygen had misused its monopoly power, exploiting the community by charging excessive prices, then British Oxygen would almost certainly have been nationalised by the government to protect the community.

One reason for taking an industry into public ownership is to protect the community from being exploited. But what if the government of the day has other ideas?

In the early eighties the British Gas Board was increasing its prices to domestic consumers each year by a substantial amount above the rate of inflation, in line with government instructions. For the financial year to March 1983, for example, its profits were enormous. On a conventional historic-cost accounting basis, its profits were probably £1.6 billion. British Gas depressed profit figures by using a current-cost accounting basis, to a current-cost profit of £660 million after paying a gas levy to the government of £530 million.

Here a government instructed a community-owned national industry to increase its prices each year substantially above inflation, and then collected a good deal of the resulting profits by means of a levy. The government was in effect using British Gas to collect a special tax from its customers.

The government was able to do so because gas was then much cheaper than electricity, and the government forced British Gas to increase its prices to near the electricity costs. The resulting profits were enormous.

To me it seems that this is a clear example of exploitation of consumers by misuse of monopoly power by a government.

Accountability to the Community

Directors and chief executives of nationalised enterprises or industries are appointed by the government of the day.

The Board of Directors is responsible for the day-to-day operation of the enterprise or industry it controls, and the directors are generally accountable for the quality of their work to those who appointed them.

The Minister who appointed them lays down the overall policy which they need to adhere to, and in the end have to adhere to, if they wish to be reappointed. In this way the Board's role becomes that of putting into effect the politically biased policies of the government of the day and so the government's policies are imposed on the nationalised enterprise or industry.

In practice the Minister can blame the board for the resulting problems but they are unlikely to be able to criticise the policies of the government.

It might be argued that the appointees are responsible through those ministers who appointed them, and thus through the government of the day, to the policy making delegate body such as Parliament. But this method of accountability is so remote from what is actually happening that it does not work effectively.

Consider what happened to British Leyland:

British Leyland was formed in 1968 by merging British car manufacturers with the intention of creating an enterprise big enough to compete effectively with foreign car manufacturers.

British Leyland (BL) was producing roughly 850,000 cars a year in the UK with 190,000 employees world-wide, making a pre-tax profit of about £40 million each year, from 1968 to 1973.

But 1973 to 1975 production dropped to 600,000 cars a year, profit turned into a loss of £90 million, and the government took control of BL in 1975.

Management became tougher, more authoritarian. Confrontation developed between workforce and management. Production continued to fall and an initial profit of £70 million had by 1980 turned into a loss of £390 million. There were massive redundancies. By 1982, BL's workforce had been reduced to 110,000 employees and the loss had been reduced to £100 million.

What had gone wrong?

Between 1968 and 1982 about £2.2 billions of taxpayers' money were poured into BL in the form of new share capital. The time taken from drawing-board to consumer had increased from three to five years. A model built under licence from a foreign company was launched in 1981.

Market share can be defined as the sales achieved by one enterprise in an industry, expressed as a percentage of total sales in that industry. It is an indication of relative success between competitors and roughly independent of the state of the economy.

Now consider this. In 1968 BL's UK market share was about 40 per cent. From 1972 BL's UK market share dropped until ten years later it had fallen to 19 per cent, and this process continued.

Summarising:

1968	Production	850,000
	Profit (GBP mill)	40
	Employees	190,000
	Market Share (%)	40

In Between:

- Taxpayers pour in £2.2 billion to keep the company going.
- Market share drops and continues to drop.
- So production drops and profits turn into increasing losses.
- Massive redundancies.

1982	Production	400,000
	Profit (GBP mill)	-100 (Loss)
	Employees	110,000
	Market Share (%)	19

Compare the figures:

	1968	1982
Production	850,000	400,000
Profit (GBP mill)	40	-100 (Loss)
Employees	190,000	110,000
Market Share (%)	40	19

The market share dropped and continued to drop, for ten long years. This situation surely requires an explanation.

How come the informed press and media failed to get across to the general public the points being made here? To the general public which was paying these enormous sums to keep the company going and who surely had the right to know how their investments were being applied and how the company was performing as a result.

What is needed is direct accountability to the community for performance in achieving the community's aims and objectives.

Political Reasons for Privatising

Large-scale privatising has been carried out in recent years for reasons which at times appear unsound and misleading. A political party, or government, may believe that private profit is more important than service to the community or the welfare of the community, of people. They would then privatise for the sake of private profit regardless of the cost to the community.

We have been told, for example, that privatising is necessary because 'government' cannot afford to support financially the community-owned industry. Those who put forward such ideas usually ignore the value of the social benefits obtained by the community from the service provided by the community-owned enterprise.

One example of such considerations is the REMPLOY enterprise, which was discussed earlier. Another clear example can be seen in arguments about what is happening to the British National Health Service. 'Unable to support financially' is not a valid argument for privatising unless social benefits and social costs are included in the cost-benefit analysis.

Another reason for high subsidies being required may well be that policy is being decided by politicians from the point of view of preconceived ideas instead of being decided on the basis of the real situation and the community's needs. It is also possible that senior management may be unable to implement policies imposed from above.

In addition, it appears that enterprises and industries may be privatised without the community getting its money back, that is sold at a loss. That is without getting back the money put in by the community while rescuing or supporting the enterprise or industry. Privatising at a loss when there is no need to sell would seem to amount to subsidising the new owners, handing public money to them.

Another reason for privatising may be to use the resulting funds for financing tax cuts so as to win an election or redistribute income and wealth from bottom wage-earners to the rich. Tax cuts hardly benefit the bottom 95 per cent of the population to any extent but the top 5 per cent gain much and very much. Using income from sale of community-owned enterprises, from privatising, in this way amounts to selling much which belongs to all, and then giving the proceeds to those who are already well-off or rich.

Conclusions

We have seen that there are good reasons for nationalising an enterprise or an industry, based on providing better service and high quality goods where needed and on the need to protect the community from exploitation.

Rolls-Royce, for example, was taken into public ownership when insolvent and returned to private ownership as a successful enterprise.

But there are political parties and governments to whom private profit is more important than service to the community and who privatise community-owned industries and enterprises regardless of the cost to the community.

From the point of view of the community there is great need to take community ownership in all its aspects out of this political tug-of-war situation.

Community ownership and nationalisation are essential ingredients of economic policy and must not be abused for the sake of private profit.

We need to make people aware of

- Aims and objectives of community ownership and nationalising, while stressing the crucial importance of

- Service to the community,
- Grassroots control by the community, and
- Accountability to the community, combined with
- Open policy-making and
- Open decision-making.

Notes and References

Notes

<1> This section owes much to {1}

References

{1} Organisations at Work
     M R Frampton, R T Norrie, A J Rees
     Nelson, 1983

{2} Community Economics: Principles
     Manfred Davidmann, 1992, 1996
     solhaam.org

{3} See chapter 7,
     'Exporting and Importing of Employment and Unemployment'
     Manfred Davidmann

Chapter 5

Ownership and Deciding Policy:
Companies, Shareholders, Directors and Community

Summary

A short statement which describes the system by which a company's majority shareholders decide policy and control the company.

Companies (Corporations)

A public company can have an unlimited number of shareholders. Its shares are available to the public and are quoted on the stock exchange. Shareholders benefit from limited liability which means that after they have paid for their shares they are not responsible for the company's debts. {6}

Allocating Profits

Some of the profits are paid out to shareholders as dividends and some are retained in the company by allocating them to reserves.

The value of a company's shares depends on its assets and its prospects. If you own 5 per cent of the company's share capital then 5 per cent of its assets belong to you. Any change in the company's assets is reflected in the value of its shares. When profits are retained by a company then this increases its assets which in turn increases the value of each share. An increase in the value of a share is called a capital gain.

So shareholders benefit from profits paid out as dividends and also from capital gains. Dividends are received each year and capital gain is realised when the shares are sold. <1>

Ownership

Ownership is the right to possess something and to decide what is to be done with it. If I own something it belongs to me and I decide what is to be done with it. An example would be owning a house.

Possession is having something in one's custody as distinct from owning it. If I possess something it belongs to another but I can decide how to use it. An example would be renting a house.

Ownership and Control by Majority Shareholder(s)

Shareholders can elect a board of directors, usually based on one vote per share. A shareholder who owns a majority of a company's voting shares has a controlling interest. His vote decides who, apart from himself or his representative, is appointed to the board of directors and so determines the policy of the business. This applies also when a few shareholders together own the majority.

Hence other shareholders usually have little say or interest in deciding policy or in the running of the company. What is left for them to decide is whether to sell the shares they hold or whether to buy more.

So the majority shareholder has in effect taken possession of the ownership rights of the other shareholders and can use the company's assets for his own ends.

Maximising Profits

Shareholders would like profits to be maximised in the short term (dividends) and long term (capital gain and security). And directors take such decisions on behalf of the controlling shareholders and decide how to divide profits between dividends and reserves (capital gain).

In practice directors are generally required by man-made laws to act first and foremost in the interests of the owners, so that it is profit which is maximised. Short-term and long-term profits can be and are being maximised regardless of the cost to others, that is regardless of the cost to the community. {2}

Profits can be increased by reducing labour costs, for example. Those wishing to increase profits regardless of the cost to others, will thus aim to reduce the standard of living of the working population, will aim to increase the needs of the working population so that people will work for less. {2-3, 5}

Decision-making: Company, Directors, Employees

A company (Co. Ltd, PLC, corporation) {6} is apparently a legal fiction. In law it is an entity which can be sued in a court, or sue others, for matters such as money owed or breach of contract. Although a company does not take decisions it can be held responsible and can be held to account for decisions taken by individuals. To that extent it serves as a cover for those who take the decisions.

Note that a 'company' cannot act. It is individuals who act, who are responsible and so accountable for the policies they decide on or omit to decide on, for the decisions they take or omit to take, for what they do or omit to do, and for the resulting consequences.

Owners appoint directors to take decisions on behalf of the owners. Directors in turn appoint senior managers to have the decisions carried out. A company's employees are employed to put into effect policies decided by its directors.

Hence it would seem to be owners and directors who are responsible and who should be held accountable for actions of the company. {2}

Motivation and Pay of Directors

Directors aim to maximise profits, are not motivated by job satisfaction, are motivated by pay in its various forms, by greater wealth and by greater influence, patronage, power. {4-5, 7}

And so directors are motivated to expand the enterprise they control by diversifying into other related areas, by taking over other enterprises, to improve profit performance.

For some time now pay of directors has been what the market will bear. It is the maximum amount the controlling shareholders will not object to in the light of dividends they receive and the increase in the value of the shares they own. It is what owners decide to pay themselves.

Work and Pay: Owners, Directors, Employees, Community

The National Remuneration Pattern {1} is a precise pictorial record of the differentials within a country, from top to bottom, from young to old. It shows the relative value placed on different kinds of work. At the top are the owners or those who work directly for them, at the bottom is the mass of wage-earners.

The pattern of differentials shows that what is rewarded is service to the owners and their directors (establishment) rather than ability and service to the community. {1}

To owners and employers the worth of a job is what has to be paid to get it done. They want work to be done at the lowest rate at which they can get it done.

Notes and References

Notes

<1> When a company is unprofitable, then dividend payments can be missed and shares can lose their value.

References

{1} Work and Pay, Incomes and Differentials:
Employer, Employee and Community
Manfred Davidmann, 1981-1995, 2007
solhaam.org

{2} Social Responsibility, Profits and Social
Accountability.
Incidents, Disasters and Catastrophes.
The Worldwide Struggle for Social Accountability.
Community Aims and Community Leadership.
Manfred Davidmann, 1979, 1995
solhaam.org

{3} 'Management and Leadership:
Local, National, Multinational (Global),
Principles and Practice'
Manfred Davidmann
ISBN 978-0-85192-057-3
See chapter 2: 'Style of Management and
Leadership'

{4} 'Management and Leadership:
Local, National, Multinational (Global),
Principles and Practice'
Manfred Davidmann
ISBN 978-0-85192-057-3
See chapter 4: 'Motivation'

{5} See chapter 16:
'The Will to Work: What People Struggle to Achieve'
Manfred Davidmann

{6} See chapter 3:
'Ownership and Limited Liability'
Manfred Davidmann

{7} 'Cooperatives and Cooperation:
Causes of Failure, Guidelines for Success'
Manfred Davidmann
ISBN 978-0-85192-056-6
See chapter 5.3: 'Building Societies'

Chapter 6

Multinational Summits and Agreements, Top-level Decision-making and Democracy

Summary

Recently negotiated top-level trading agreements appear to be taking control over key aspects of the internal affairs of participating countries, taking control away from elected governments, giving the control to multinational corporations and top-level organisations.

The information given here was extracted largely from two reports {1, 2}, part of a study undertaken to explore why people have to struggle throughout their adult lives, in all countries and organisations, at all levels, to maintain and improve their standard of living and quality of life. We know what people are struggling to achieve {3, 4} and the study was undertaken to explore why people have to struggle by looking at what they are struggling against <1>.

Participative Organisation: The Meaning of 'Democracy' <2>

Participative (democratic) organisation {2} rests on the population electing representatives, on the basis of each person having one vote.

Representatives are responsible to, and accountable to, the population for putting into effect policies decided by the population.

What underlies participative organisation (democracy) is decision-taking by the people at the level of the people.

What needs to be stressed is that in a participative (democratic) organisation policies are decided by a well-informed population at the level of the population and that these policies then become binding on management or government. <3>

And representatives, governments or government officials do not have the authority or right to reduce or sign away the participative (democratic) rights of the electors, of the population.

In an authoritarian organisation the policy decisions are taken at the top or near the top by the hierarchy (establishment) and are binding on the organisation's members. Decision-taking at the top is sometimes referred to as 'deciding centrally'. Authoritarian organisation is the opposite of democracy and underlies dictatorship.

What we see all around us is conflict between authoritarian minds wishing to dominate, control and exploit on the one hand and, on the other hand, citizens wishing to maintain and improve the standard of living and quality of life for the population as a whole by democratic (grassroots level) decision-taking.

What we see is top-level leaderships trying to take over decision-taking from the population.

So the real struggle is not between political left and right, but is a struggle for participation (the right to take decisions).

Agreements between Top-level Leaderships

Top-level leaderships by agreements between themselves and without proper democratic authority for doing so, are apparently attempting to take over decision-taking from the population, are attempting in this way to negate democratic decision-taking.

The 'General Agreement on Tariffs and Trade' (GATT)

GATT is a treaty between many countries in which they agreed that changed and new life-forms can be owned by multinational corporations, generation after generation. {5}

The GATT agreement apparently gives exclusive protection to patent holders for 20 years and imposes strict enforcement criteria. Huge royalty payments will have to be made to multinational corporations. 'Astonishingly, the rules place the onus of proof in case of dispute on the farmers, a provision going against normal rules of justice' {7}. The resulting costs could prevent the vast mass of small farmers from disputing the source of the seeds they are using. {5}

So multinational corporations have been given ownership over new life-forms and the power to force farmers worldwide to pay the multinational each year for seeds even when these seeds were grown by the farmer the previous year. {5}

It appears that GATT serves the interests of multinationals, that is of those who own and control them, at the expense of the economic and social interests and welfare of individual countries, of their people, of their citizens. {5}

And that a situation has been created in which the nature of profit-motivated and profit-orientated multinationals threatens human independence and freedom. {5}

In 1998 a US multinational 'announced plans to unravel the entire human genetic code by 2001', saying it intended to patent 'the most valuable gene sequences', and to sell the information to scientific institutions and drug companies. {8}

Combining this information with recent developments concerning the cloning of animals and human beings raises disturbing and even fearful prospects.

'Ownership' has been defined as 'the right to possess an item of property' and so one has to look closely at where the right comes from and how it is exercised.

Ownership rights are the property of a country's citizens and communities {9, 10}. No elected representative, government or government employee has overriding fundamental authority to hand over to multinational corporations (that is to those who own and control them {11}), or to anyone else, such ownership rights.

So it would seem that the patent provisions of the GATT agreement are big-business-serving and arbitrary. {9, 5}

The 'Multilateral Agreement on Investment' (MAI)

MAI stands for 'Multilateral Agreement on Investment'. But its name does not reflect those aspects which are of deep concern. What is disturbing are not only the provisions of this proposed treaty but also that the provisions were debated in almost complete secrecy.

It appears that representatives of multinationals and governments representing the 29 richest industrialised countries, all OECD members, had been developing the MAI's provisions at the OECD (Organisation for Economic Co-operation and Development) since 1995. This seems to have been done in complete secrecy till a leaked copy became available on the Internet in 1997.

It seems that the agreement was to have been finalised in February 1998. Apparently it was adverse publicity relating to its restrictive provisions which delayed completion as concerned groups of citizens publicised their concerns. And some governments have now withdrawn their support.

So let us look at the kind of provisions this almost-agreed agreement on 'Multilateral Agreement on Investment' contained {12, 13}:

Democratically elected governments

1. Would have had to allow multinationals access to the country.
2. Would have been prevented from discriminating against foreign firms, would not be able to refuse any form of investment in any sector apart from defence.
3. Would have been prevented from reducing or controlling a multinational's profits, say by minimum-wage or anti-pollution legislation, or by legislation to ensure local employment.

Multinationals would have had the right to

1. Sue national governments for any profits lost through laws which discriminated against the multinational, and which harmed a multinational's interests.
2. Sue national governments in an international court which would have been closed to public scrutiny.

We saw that multinationals can legally avoid paying corporation tax by transfer pricing {15} and that unitary taxation <4> {14, 15} can overcome this tax avoidance by assessing the actual profits being generated by a multinational in a particular country. Multinationals could, under MAI, have refused to be taxed by a system of unitary taxation.

Socially responsible and caring governmental legislation has to take precedence over the profit-motivated activities of corporations.

But it appears that under MAI the national governments would have handed over control, that is authority to act, over much of the economic and social welfare of their citizens to multinational corporations, that is to those who own and direct these corporations {11}, if they had agreed to this treaty.

In other words, multinationals would have been given overriding authority over democratically elected governments.

Conclusions

Authoritarian Struggle to Take Over and Control Decision-taking by Transferring it to Leaders

Authoritarian minds attempt to take over and place democratically controlled organisations under authoritarian control. They do so by struggling to take over the decision-taking in the management and control of companies, enterprises and all types of community organisations.

We can see the struggle in all organisations and at all levels. It is a struggle against authoritarian management or government for the right to take decisions. And in all democratic organisations it is a struggle against the authoritarian mind taking over the decision-taking.

A continuous battle is taking place between on the one hand policy-deciding by the many through elected assemblies, and on the other hand policy-deciding at the top, by a few. This is clearly shown by the way in which full-time officials and executives attempt to take power away from their policy-setting assemblies, after which they attempt to impose their will on the membership or population.

The government's role of keeping the system in operation and of transferring vast funds from the working population to leaderships {1}, explains the intense struggle going on within political parties for control of decision-taking (policy-setting), with authoritarian minds attempting to concentrate decision-taking in the hands of the top-level party leadership.

These attempts to take over and control decision-taking processes are far more one-sided than would be the case if we were looking at unrelated chance events, at unrelated local struggles. At times the pattern seems progressive as if it were planned.

Agreements between Top-level Leaderships

Recently negotiated top-level trading agreements (GATT and the proposed MAI) appear to be taking away the control over key aspects of the internal affairs of participating countries. Taking control away from their elected governments, giving the control to multinational corporations.

It appears that the 'General Agreement on Tariffs and Trade' (GATT) serves the interests of multinationals, that is of those who own and control them, at the expense of the economic and social interests and welfare of individual countries, of their people, of their citizens. {5}

And it would seem that the patent provisions of the GATT agreement are big-business-serving and arbitrary. {5, 9}

MAI stands for 'Multilateral Agreement on Investment'. But its name does not reflect those aspects which are of deep concern.

What is disturbing are not only the provisions of this proposed treaty but also that the provisions were debated in complete secrecy till a leaked copy became available on the Internet in 1997.

It appears that under MAI the national governments would have handed over control, that is authority to act, over much of the economic and social welfare of their citizens to multinational corporations (that is to those who own and direct these corporations), if they had agreed to this treaty.

In other words, multinationals would have been given overriding authority over democratically elected governments.

And that a situation has been created in which the nature of profit-motivated and profit-orientated multinationals threatens human independence and freedom. {5}

Socially responsible and caring governmental legislation has to take precedence over the profit-motivated activities of corporations.

Secrecy and Publicity

We saw that the MAI's provisions were discussed in complete secrecy and that it was adverse publicity relating to its restrictive provisions which delayed completion of the MAI as concerned groups of citizens publicised their concerns. We also saw that consequently some governments withdrew support.

A company, corporation, multinational organisation or meeting, can serve as a front behind which those who take key decisions can hide, as a front for owners, directors or top-level individuals.

All multinational and so-called 'summit' meetings are suspect. Suspect are also multinational, international, global organisations, too often run by unelected self-perpetuating hierarchies, holding secretive meetings arriving at secretive social, economic or military agreements and treaties.

Social Struggle, Aims and Action

So profits and power are apparently being maximised regardless of the cost to others, to the community. Without care or concern for the condition, standard of living or quality of life of the working population. Without being concerned about the enormous human suffering which results.

What we see are consequences of decisions made at the top, and the results of putting them into effect. Results and consequences which at times make the decisions seem so brutal that they appear inhuman.

What underlies democracy is decision-taking by the people at the level of the people. But what we see is top-level leaderships trying to take over decision-taking from the population.

Secretive top-level multinational meetings and agreements negate democratic government and decision-taking, without having overriding authority or right to do so.

But representatives, governments or government officials do not have the authority or right to override, reduce or sign away the participative (democratic) rights of the electors, of the population.

No elected representative, government or government employee has overriding right or authority

1. to hand over to corporations (that is to those who own and control them), to any other organisation or to anyone else, an overriding control over the present and future, economic and social, welfare of the people, or
2. to sign away democratic rights of their people for the self-determination of key fundamental aspects of their lives.

Decision-taking by leaderships has to be replaced by decision-making at the level of the people.

The real struggle is not between political left and right, but is a struggle for participation (the right to make decisions).

Leaderships fear bad publicity, fear public awareness of socially irresponsible behaviour and consequent impact on sales and market share, on an individual's career or on an organisation's reputation and credibility.

So an effective control of corporate and top-level irresponsibility is publicity of what is being planned or being done, making the public aware of who did or is doing what, and of who condoned or omitted to restrain, antisocial or antidemocratic activities.

Particularly so when publicity names those responsible for making antisocial decisions, and those responsible for condoning, or for omitting to restrain, antisocial activities.

References and Notes

Notes

<1>   See {1-2, 9, 14, 16}.

<2>   Extracted from {2} which discusses the meaning of democracy, and its necessary requirements, in more detail.

<3>   See also {6} for a more comprehensive discussion of the electing, appointing and appraisal of managers, directors and elected representatives, the right to know, the right to be heard, and of work, pay and differentials.

<4>   In {14} see 'Condoning Tax Avoidance by the Rich.'

References

{ 1}   See chapter 10:
'What People are Struggling Against: How Society is Organised for Controlling and Exploiting People'
Manfred Davidmann

{ 2}   See chapter 11:
        'Democracy Under Attack: Top-level Leadership
        and Decision-making'
        Manfred Davidmann

{ 3}   'Management and Leadership:
        Local, National, Multinational (Global),
        Principles and Practice'
        Manfred Davidmann
        ISBN 978-0-85192-057-3
        See chapter 4: 'Motivation'

{ 4}   See chapter 16:
        'The Will to Work: What People Struggle to
        Achieve'
        Manfred Davidmann

{ 5}   See chapter 9:
        'Creating, Patenting and Marketing of New Forms
        of Life'
        Manfred Davidmann

{ 6}   'Cooperatives and Cooperation:
        Causes of Failure, Guidelines for Success'
        Manfred Davidmann
        ISBN 978-0-85192-056-6

{ 7}   Seeds of discontent
        Walter Schwarz
        Guardian, 11/03/94

{ 8}   US company plans to patent key gene codes
        Paul Brown and Martin Walker
        Guardian, 13/05/98

{ 9}   See chapter 12:
        'Understanding How Society is Organised for
        Controlling and Exploiting People'
        Manfred Davidmann

{10}   See chapter 2:
        'Ownership'
        Manfred Davidmann

{11}   See chapter 5:
         'Ownership and Deciding Policy: Companies,
         Shareholders, Directors and Community'
         Manfred Davidmann

{12}   Globalisers run into the buffers
         Larry Elliott and Charlotte Denny
         Guardian, 24/03/98

{13}   Move to revive world pact
         Larry Elliott
         Guardian, 10/09/98

{14}   See chapter 13:
         'Taxing the Population for Private Profit'
         Manfred Davidmann

{15}   See chapter 8:
         'Transfer Pricing and Taxation'
         Manfred Davidmann

{16}   See chapter 14:
         'Corrupted Economics and Misguided (Misleading)
         Experts'
         Manfred Davidmann

Chapter 7

Exporting and Importing of Employment and Unemployment

Summary

This report discusses both exporting and importing of employment and unemployment, the underlying principles and the effect of trade between low-wage and high-wage countries.

It shows what is required to halt and reverse the trend towards increasing unemployment and falling living standards in high-wage countries.

The report not only shows what is required to make the system work, but also the controls required to prevent misuse of the system and to protect people.

There are sections about transferring operations abroad, about importing from low-wage countries, about social costs of unemployment, about community objectives and community support for enterprises, about ownership rights and about ensuring that the behaviour of enterprises is socially responsible.

CAUSES OF UNEMPLOYMENT

We are here looking at main causes of unemployment, namely

1. Replacing people with labour-saving equipment such as computers and robots (increasing productivity, impact of technology).

2. Transferring manufacturing and service work from a high-wage home country to low-wage countries.

3. Importing goods and services which originate in low-wage countries, into a high-wage home country.

Computers and Robots (Increasing Productivity, Impact of Technology)

Computers

Application of computers in offices, and the computerising of production equipment, replaced and is replacing people. Productivity and profits increase but unemployment rises.

Robots

It is some time ago that a Japanese Trade Union suggested that 'robots should pay income tax'.

It would, of course, be the enterprise which would pay the tax. In other words, employers should pay the social costs of the unemployment created by a robot doing work done previously by people or doing work which could be done by people.

Transferring Operations Abroad

Exporting Employment and Importing Unemployment

Take an enterprise owned by British owners, employing British capital, employing British employees in Britain. Wage rates are much lower in the Far East because of the low standard of living of those living there. So the British enterprise (owners, directors) transfers some or all of its production (or other) operations to a Far Eastern country. And this applies to calculators, computers, television sets, electrical and electronic equipment, toys, and much else.

Their British employees are made redundant, are dismissed, become unemployed. But employment increases in the Far Eastern country. And all this for the sake of greater profits to owners and directors of the British enterprise.

Employment increases abroad and decreases in Britain, so that employment has been exported. Unemployment decreases abroad but increases in Britain, so that unemployment has been imported. Employment has been exported, unemployment has been imported, and all this for the sake of private profit.

The large additional profits which result from transferring operations abroad then do not result from doing a better job, or from providing better, or more needed, or more effectively produced, goods or services. These additional profits result from importing unemployment into the UK, are the result of dismissing their British employees.

The social costs of unemployment, however, are in the end paid by the unemployed (who are part of the community) and to some extent by the community as a whole. So the enterprise has passed on to the community this part of its operating costs, is making a profit at the expense of the community.

The social costs of an operation have to be paid by the enterprise, the social costs of unemployment have to be paid by the enterprise which caused the unemployment. {1}

To the extent to which an enterprise fails to allow for the social costs of its operations, to that extent are its profits derived from passing its operating costs to the community, is it making profits at the expense of the community, is it exploiting the community and its members.

Importing Employment and Exporting Unemployment

As far as I know, Switzerland for many years successfully exported unemployment. Foreign workers may be employed in Switzerland only if no Swiss national is available for doing the work. And apparently foreign workers may stay in Switzerland only while having work.

So it seems that Switzerland is increasing employment in Switzerland by importing labour when required and only while required. They are exporting unemployment by insisting that foreign workers leave for their home countries when the employment terminates or when a Swiss national is available for doing it. They are importing employment, are exporting unemployment.

In such circumstances the social costs of unemployment are passed on to other communities. In effect the social costs of unemployment carried by these communities is reduced by an amount corresponding to the period of employment abroad.

Importing Goods and Services which Originate in a Low-wage Country, into a High-wage Home-country

It would seem that importing cheaper goods from low-wage countries results in cheaper goods being made available, in lower prices. But we need to consider that middlemen take excessive profits, that unemployment increases, that wages and living standards decrease. And these are the social costs arising from such importing operations.

The consumer experiences a small lowering of prices from such imports, an apparent gain to the community. The picture changes when the larger costs to the community are included which the community (including consumers) has to pay.

Goods and services are bought cheaply in low-wage countries and sold in high-wage countries, at what seem to be large and excessive profit mark-ups.

Prices used to be based on 'cost plus reasonable mark-up', and unhindered competition was meant to ensure that the mark-up was reasonable. Prices are now based on what people can be persuaded to pay for what they can be persuaded to buy. The mark-up between producing in a low-wage country, and then selling in a high-wage country, can be enormous.

So imports are priced at what the market will bear, or just under. Sales of home-produced product reduce or its prices are lowered so as to compete with the imported product. The importer can easily afford to reduce his prices a little further, and so on until, in the end, the home-country's production facilities are knocked out. In the home-country we see prices reduced a little as long as low-wage countries compete with each other, increasing unemployment and reducing wages in the home-country.

This process looks like the free-market system in operation. However, what is actually happening is very different.

Underlying the free-market system {1} is that unhindered balancing of supply and demand, that is unhindered competition, ensures that goods and services are made available at reasonable prices, at reasonable profit margins. As supply and demand change so the profit margin changes and it is this profit change which produces balance.

The system functions in this way as long as wage rates and living standard are held at constant level, remain roughly at the same level.

In practice we see an enormous difference in wages between low-wage and high-wage countries which results in large profits. These profits are almost unaffected by supply and demand changes. Hence there is no effective competition for this product, the requirement for unhindered competition has not been satisfied and the system fails to meet the community's needs.

Profit tends to be the sole consideration, regardless of the consequences to the community, regardless of the cost to people. Instead of producing more effectively and competitively at home, owners and directors find it easier and more profitable to import from low-wage countries. Unemployment increases and increasing unemployment and social need is used to force down wages and living standards.

Owners and directors in this way profit from the unemployment and the lower standard of living their operations cause in the home-country. They will continue to profit from increasing unemployment and its consequences as long as they do not have to pay the social costs of their operations. In other words, as long as they are allowed to pass this part of their operating costs to the community.

Social Costs of Unemployment

The fundamental principles of the free-market system are discussed at some length in 'Community Economics: Principles' {1}. The real profit or gain any enterprise achieves is the gain the community obtains as a result of the enterprises' operations. Thus the social costs, that is the costs to the community of any operation, have to be taken into account when assessing the gain resulting from that operation {2}.

The social costs of unemployment to people as individuals, to their families, and to the community as a whole, are:

> INDIVIDUALS
>> Poverty, lack of spending money
>> Frustration, despair
>> Young people without full-time work experience
>> Social disillusionment
>> Ill health
>> Reduced life span
>> Mental illness
>> Increasing suicide rate
>> Drug abuse, crime

FAMILIES
> Increased family breakup
> Homelessness
> Domestic violence

COMMUNITY
> Higher and rising crime rates
> Brutalisation of lifestyle
> Lost Income:
>> (1) Loss of income tax from those now unemployed.
>> (2) Loss of National Insurance contributions which would have been received from both employees and employers.
>> (3) Loss of Value Added Tax as the unemployed reduce their spending.
> Increased Expenditure
>> (4) Increased cost of Unemployment Benefit (Among developed countries, the British rate of benefit appears to be one of the lowest).
>> (5) Increased cost of Social Security support payments.
>> (6) Increased costs for Health Service, Police and Prisons.

Note that persistent lack of care and consideration towards its members leads to a view of society as being hostile and unrewarding {3}. We now see this taking place and see its effects.

The social cost of unemployment to the community is the total cost to the community, is the sum of all the items listed here.

Unemployment, Wages and Profits

Unemployment has increased to an unacceptable level as a result of allowing owners and directors to replace people by equipment and to import unemployment, all for the sake of private profit.

What is being said on behalf of owners and directors is that increasing and high rates of unemployment are desirable (from the point of view of owners and directors). High levels of unemployment enable owners and directors to reduce opposition within their employees because of the harsh consequences of dismissal. And high levels of unemployment also enable owners and directors to force down wage rates and salaries, and to reduce conditions of employment, as people struggle and compete with each other to obtain employment.

The underlying political ideology would appear to be well outlined by statements like 'rising unemployment is needed to bring down wage settlements', countered by statements like 'using rising unemployment to frighten people into accepting low wage increases'.

So higher unemployment enables the employer to force wages down, to reduce labour costs, to increase profits.

It seems that under such conditions unemployment, and the causes of unemployment, are not being tackled effectively. Unacceptable high levels of unemployment and the suffering this brings are being explained away by side-tracking dead-end theorising.

There would appear to be no valid reason why owners and directors of enterprises should be allowed to profit from creating unemployment for the sake of greater private profits.

Principles

In 'COMMUNITY ECONOMICS: Principles' {1} we looked at the purpose of enterprises and profit-motivation.

We saw that the social costs, that is the costs to the community of any operation by an enterprise, have to be paid by the enterprise.

We saw that for the free-market economic system to work, it is essential that prices are allowed to float unhindered according to the unhindered natural balance between supply and demand, within limits set to protect the community.

This means {1} that there must be free unhindered competition.

It also means {1} that profit margins and prices need to be controlled effectively so as to protect the community from exploitation.

Underlying the free-market system {1} is that unhindered balancing of supply and demand, that is unhindered competition, ensures that goods and services are made available at reasonable prices, at reasonable profit margins. As supply and demand change so the profit margin changes and it is this profit change which produces balance.

The system functions in this way but only as long as wage rates and living standard are held at constant level, remain roughly at the same level.

Prices used to be based on 'cost plus reasonable mark-up', and unhindered competition was meant to ensure that the mark-up was reasonable. Prices are now based on what people can be persuaded to pay for what they can be persuaded to buy.

We see <1> an enormous difference in wages between low-wage and high-wage countries which results in large profits. Goods and services are bought cheaply in low-wage countries and sold in high-wage countries, at what seem to be large and excessive profit mark-ups. These profits are almost unaffected by supply and demand changes. Hence there is no effective competition for this product and the system fails to meet the community's needs.

Further reductions of living standards in high-wage countries are quite unacceptable. Indeed, this process has gone too far already and needs to be reversed.

And this means that profits between producer and consumer have to be limited, regulated and controlled. Enterprises must pay to the community the social costs of their operations. Tariffs are needed to protect home industries, employment and living standards.

No matter which way you look at it, it is better and it is in our interest that wages and living standards in low-wage countries increase to our levels, and not the other way about.

Community Support and Ownership Rights

As citizens, people are not rewarded for behaving responsibly towards others and towards the community, are not rewarded for keeping the community's laws, and neither should enterprises. So enterprises {1} should not be rewarded for socially responsible behaviour.

And an enterprise should be punished {1}, just like an ordinary person, when the enterprise's behaviour is socially irresponsible.

There may be occasions when it is in the interests of the community to pay part of an enterprise's social costs, to subsidise the enterprise, to support it in some way.

No investor, that is 'owner', would give his money to some ailing enterprise without an appropriate return. Indeed, the greater the risk or need, the greater the return demanded.

Hence if the community gives direct or indirect support to an enterprise, industry or section of the economy, then a corresponding amount of the voting share capital needs to be transferred to community ownership.

This applies equally well to providing subsidies, grants, tax exemptions, capital allowances and other direct or indirect inducements to foreign enterprises for them to establish production or other operations in our home-country.

Transferring voting share capital to community ownership raises the important point about who exercises control. It is the community which should exercise control and not some distant government, management or union appointee.

The voting rights should be divided equally and given direct to each employee, with employees voting as individuals. They should also be entitled to and enabled to elect one or more directors from among themselves, whose role would be to represent the interests of the community and to report back to the employees and to the community any matter of interest to the employees or to the community.

Community Objectives

(Compiled largely from other pages of this report)

1. The social costs, that is the costs to the community of any operation by an enterprise, have to be paid by the enterprise. This is a basic and essential requirement. The social costs of unemployment have to be paid by the enterprise which caused the unemployment. {1}

   Note that persistent lack of care and consideration towards its members leads to a view of society as being hostile and unrewarding {3}. We now see this taking place and see its effects.

   The social cost of unemployment to the community is its total cost to the community, is the sum of all the items listed here. <2>

2. For the free-market economic system to work, it is essential that prices are allowed to float unhindered according to the unhindered natural balance between supply and demand, within limits set to protect the community.

   Which means that there must be free unhindered competition. {1}

   And that profit margins and prices need to be controlled effectively so as to protect the community from exploitation. {1}

In practice <1> we see an enormous difference in wages between low-wage and high-wage countries which results in large profits. These profits are almost unaffected by supply and demand changes. Hence there is no effective competition for this product.

As a result the system fails to meet the community's needs, unemployment increases in the high-wage country and living standards drop.

3. Further reductions of living standards in high-wage countries are quite unacceptable. Indeed, this process has gone too far already and needs to be reversed. And this means that profits between producer and consumer have to be limited, regulated and controlled.

Enterprises must pay to the community the social costs of their operations. Tariffs and possibly surcharges and other means of restricting imports are needed to protect home industries, employment and living standards.

No matter which way you look at it, it is better and it is in our interest that wages and living standards in low-wage countries increase to our levels, and not the other way about.

We should find ways of encouraging and supporting measures which would increase the level of wages, the standard of living and the quality of life of the working population in low-wage countries.

One way may be the setting up of production or service operations in low-wage countries, producing or providing services there.

4. Home enterprises, industries and services need to be protected by controlling the large and excessive profits taken from imports from low-wage countries.

This refers to profit from the point of origin to the final point of sale, including both.

Profit and profit margins need to be strictly controlled, laying down rules for profit calculation and number of middlemen.

A formidable task made possible by available computing technology once the basic guidelines have been determined.

5. Socially irresponsible behaviour has to be unprofitable behaviour. Conditions need to be changed so that socially irresponsible behaviour results in severe losses.

    Enterprises, like ordinary people, should not be rewarded for socially responsible behaviour and, just like ordinary people, enterprises should be punished when their behaviour is socially irresponsible.

    Those who profit at the expense of the community need to face severe penalties and punishment.

6. Tariffs need to allow for differences in labour costs and standard of living and also for foreign subsidies and other aid and support received by the foreign industry (producer) when it is attempting to knock out our home industry or take its market over.

    Tariffs are likely to result in foreign investment in the home-country, aimed at crossing the tariff barrier by producing in the home market. No subsidies, support or aid, such as tax exemptions, should be given. There has to be a clear legal requirement for that enterprises' product or service to have a home-country-produced content of goods, material and labour of, I would suggest, at least 80 or 85 per cent. And that home-produced content must include the high-tech content.

7. There may be occasions when it is in the interests of the community to pay part of an enterprise's social costs, to subsidise the enterprise, to support it in some way.

    No investor, that is 'owner', would give his money to some ailing enterprise without an appropriate return. Indeed, the greater the risk or need, the greater the return demanded.

    So if the community gives direct or indirect support to an enterprise, industry or section of the economy, then a corresponding amount of the voting share capital needs to be transferred to community ownership.

    This applies equally well to providing subsidies, grants, tax exemptions, capital allowances and other direct or indirect inducements to foreign enterprises for them to establish production or other operations in our home-country.

8. Transferring voting share capital to community ownership raises the important point about who exercises control. It is the community which should exercise control and not some distant civil servant or government appointee.

The voting rights should be divided equally and given direct to each employee, with employees voting as individuals. They should also be entitled to, and enabled to, elect one or more directors from among themselves, whose role would be to represent the interests of the community and to report back to the employees and to the community any matter of interest to the employees or to the community.

9. So much damage has been done by past behaviour, and so much support has been given to enterprises in the past that it seems more than reasonable for such measures as are put forward here to be implemented quickly but cautiously, and backdated.

10. The kind of society to aim at under present conditions is one in which all can work four days a week earning enough to have a high standard of living and a high quality of life.

This is both possible and achievable under present conditions.

Notes and References

Notes

<1>   See section 'Importing Goods and Services which Originate in a Low-wage Country, Into a High-wage Country'

<2>   See section 'Social Costs of Unemployment'

References

{1}   Community Economics: Principles
      Manfred Davidmann, 1992, 1996
      solhaam.org

{2}   Social Responsibility, Profits and Social
      Accountability.
      Incidents, Disasters and Catastrophes.
      The Worldwide Struggle for Social Accountability.
      Community Aims and Community Leadership.
      Manfred Davidmann, 1979, 1995
      solhaam.org

{3}   In 'Management and Leadership:
      Local, National, Multinational (Global),
      Principles and Practice'
      Manfred Davidmann
      ISBN 978-0-85192-057-3
      See chapter 4: 'Motivation'

Chapter 8

Transfer Pricing and Taxation

Summary

One of the most controversial and often least understood operations of multinationals, transfer pricing, is clearly described and defined.

An easily-followed illustration shows how transfer pricing can be used by multinationals to maximise their profits by tax avoidance and by obtaining tax rebates.

Also discussed is the effect of transfer pricing on the tax burden carried by other tax payers.

Transfer Pricing

One of the most controversial and often least understood of a multinational's operations is that of Transfer Pricing.

When one part of a multinational organisation in one country transfers (that is, sells) goods, services or know-how to another part in another country, the price charged for these goods or services is called 'transfer price'. This may be a purely arbitrary figure, meaning by this that it may be unrelated to costs incurred, may be unrelated to operations carried out or to added value. We will see here that the transfer price can be set at a level which reduces or even cancels out the total tax which has to be paid by the multinational.

Consider ourselves to be directors of the multinational. We are sitting in its boardroom at the head office in the home country of the multinational. The Finance Director is reviewing our operations.

FIG 1 Transfer Pricing

	Subsidiary Company (Fully owned and controlled by Parent Company)		Parent Company (and Head Office of the Multinational)		
	Host Country		Home Country		
	Price of Goods Bought (£)	Transfer Price (£)	Selling Price (£)	Totals (£)
Case 1	100	200	300	
Profit Before Tax (£)		100	100		200
Tax Rate (%)		20	60		
Tax Paid (£)		20	60		80
Profit After Tax (£)		80	40		120
Case 2	100	280	300	
Profit Before Tax (£)		180	20		200
Tax Rate (%)		20	60		
Tax Paid (£)		36	12		48
Profit After Tax (£)		144	8		152
Case 3	100	300	300	
Profit Before Tax (£)		200	0		200
Tax Rate (%)		20	60		
Tax Paid (£)		40	0		40
Profit After Tax (£)		160	0		160
Case 4	100	400	300	
Profit Before Tax (£)		300	-100		200
Tax Rate (%)		20	60		
Tax Paid (£)		60	- 60		0
Profit After Tax (£)		240	- 40		200
Case 5	100	500	300	
Profit Before Tax (£)		400	-200		200
Tax Rate (%)		20	60		
Tax Paid (£)		80	-120		- 40
Profit After Tax (£)		320	- 80		240

He is talking about our trade with another company in another country. We are the parent company, they are one of our subsidiary companies. This means that they belong to us, that in the end we decide what they do and do not do, what happens to their profits.

We, the parent company, are located in the 'home country'. The subsidiary company is located in another country, namely in the 'host country'.

The Finance Director is simplifying the picture for our benefit:

Paying Some Tax

Case 1

The subsidiary company buys goods at £100 each. They repack them and then export them from their country to our country, selling them to us at a price of £200 each. They are transferring them to us for a transfer price of £200.

So they have made a profit of £200-£100=£100 and we are getting them at a price of £200. This case is illustrated by Figure 1 (Case 1).

Having imported them at £200 each we sell them for £300 and thus make a profit of £300-£200=£100.

Our overall profit is thus £100 in the subsidiary company's host country and another £100 in the multinational's home country, a total of £200.

However, we need to consider the tax these companies have to pay on their profits, as the rates of tax (company or corporation tax) is different in the two countries.

The subsidiary has to pay corporation tax of 20% of the £100 profit and so the tax amounts to £20. Our home-country corporation tax is 60% of the £100 profit, and so our tax amounts to £60.

Overall, tax paid is £20+£60=£80 and this reduces our before-tax profit of £200 to an after-tax profit of £200-£80=£120.

The subsidiary contributed £80 to this profit, while our own operations contributed £40. The after-tax profit generated by us, that is by the parent company in the home country, was smaller because we paid corporation tax of 60% which compares with the subsidiary's 20%.

All the numbers given so far are illustrated by Figure 1 (Case 1). Our Finance Director points out that as the overall after-tax profit is 40% of the selling price we should be pleased with the outcome.

However, we can tell the subsidiary what to charge and can make the transfer price whatever we like. The transfer price is arbitrary, depending as it does only on agreement between ourselves and the subsidiary, and thus on ourselves.

Case 2

Consider Case 2 (see Figure 1). The transfer price is now £280 (compared with the previous £200). This has the effect of shifting before-tax profits from the parent company's home country (corporation tax 60%) to the subsidiary's host country (corporation tax 20%).

Overall, we now pay less tax (£36+£12=£48) and as the before-tax profit is unchanged (£200), the after-tax profit becomes £200-£48=£152 and that is much more than the corresponding profit of £120 we made with a transfer price of £200.

The subsidiary contributes £144 to this while our own contribution is £8.

Our overall after-tax profit is now 51% of the selling price.

Merely by changing the transfer price to an arbitrary higher figure of £280 we have increased our overall after-tax profit from £120 to £152, increased it by a staggering 27%.

Paying No Tax

Case 3

As the transfer price is arbitrary, it can be £300 (see Figure 1, Case 3). This means that we are buying and selling at the same price of £300.

Overall tax paid is now £40 and our after-tax profit becomes £160.

The subsidiary contributes £160 to this while our own contribution is £0.

So what we have done is to shift all our profits to the subsidiary and do not need to pay tax in the home country.

But we need not stop there. The parent company can shift even more of its profits to the subsidiary. It can make a loss and this is illustrated by Case 4.

Getting Tax Repayments

Case 4

This case shows what happens if the transfer price is increased to £400. The subsidiary makes a profit of £300 and we make a loss of £100 on each item.

This loss can be used by us to reduce our tax liability on other profitable operations carried out by the parent company in the home country. As a result we pay correspondingly less tax.

The subsidiary pays corporation tax of £60 on their profits while we, the parent company, reduce our tax bill by £60, in effect getting a rebate of £60.

Hence the overall result is that we pay no tax at all on this transaction and our after-tax profit becomes £200.

We can take this one step further and make the Transfer Price £500 (see Case 5).

Case 5

The subsidiary now makes a profit of £400 and we make a loss of £200.

The subsidiary pays corporation tax of £80 on their profits while we, the parent company, reduce our tax bill by £120, in effect getting a rebate of £120.

Hence the overall result is that we get a tax rebate of £120 in the home country, pay £80 corporation tax in the host country, and are thus left with a tax rebate of £40 on this transaction. Adding this to our profit increases the after-tax profit from £200 to £240.

Tax Avoidance

Tax Avoidance Increases Profits

So by increasing the purely arbitrary transfer price we doubled our after-tax profit, increasing it by 100%.

This was done without any change to our procedures, operations or added value, was done by merely changing book entries.

So where do these additional profits come from?

They arise from tax avoidance. In other words it is possible for a multinational company to minimise its liability for corporation tax by transfer pricing.

This is legal until governments legislate to prevent this practice.

But note that in the cases we discussed, the tax paid to the host-country government increased, while the tax paid to the home-country government decreased, case by case. In other words, one government's loss is the other government's gain.

So one government can be expected to want to legislate against unfair transfer pricing practices, while the other government can be expected to object to, and to resist, such legislation.

Tax Avoidance Transfers the Tax Obligation

The parent company operates in the home country. The government of that country or state spend money on behalf of its citizens - providing education, health care, social security, protection against crime and security against attack from outside. It collects much of the money it needs from citizens and companies by means of a tax on income - those who earn most pay most, those who earn least pay least. This tax is called Corporation Tax when it is collected from companies (corporations) and Income Tax when it is collected from individuals.

Say a multinational has increased its profits by tax avoidance. As the government's expenses have not changed it must make up this shortfall elsewhere. From its other tax payers, say from its citizens. So its citizens pay more tax, the government can now spend the same amount as before, the multinational's profits have increased.

In other words, the multinational's increased profits arise from money which is in effect collected by the government by taxation from its taxpayers.

The multinational, and this means the owners and directors of the multinational, are thus in effect taxing the people and in this way increasing the multinational's profits and thus their own incomes and wealth.

A matter far removed from earning reasonable profits from providing needed quality goods and services at reasonable prices in open competition with other corporations.

Many multinationals have grown to a size where they threaten or dominate the economic and financial independence and well-being of many countries. Multinationals are accountable to their directors and owners for profitability and growth instead of being accountable to elected representatives of the people for acting for or against the national interest.

Studies published in the USA, for example, tell us much about the extent to which multinationals can avoid paying tax on their profits. These present a disturbing picture.

It seems that at times some top companies pay no federal income tax or obtain an overall rebate. Tax allowances appear to add well over $100bn each year to the accounts of US corporations, and are thus given to owners and directors.

It has become common knowledge that multinational enterprises can operate against national interests.

That multinationals <1> can gain so much profit from tax avoidance, that is from in effect taxing the population, is a case in point.

Multinationals need to be made accountable to elected representatives of the people, for their policies and for acting for or against the national interest.

Notes

<1> It has become common knowledge that multinational enterprises can operate against national interests. And occasionally one sees multinationals referred to as 'transnationals' or as 'global'. The words 'transnational' and 'global' are not at present associated with antisocial operations and apparently that is why they are sometimes used as a label for a multinational.

Chapter 9

Creating, Patenting and Marketing of New Forms of Life

Summary

This report evaluates what is happening in genetic manipulation, and in the worldwide application and use of new life-forms by multinationals.

The moral and ethical questions raised are considerable, public health risks are high, and the report looks at trends from the point of view of the community.

78

Changed and new life-forms can now be owned by multinational corporations, generation after generation. The report evaluates what is happening to private ownership of life-forms as a result of the GATT agreement. It would seem that the nature of profit-orientated multinationals threatens public health, and that independence and freedom are at risk.

The report contains important far-reaching conclusions and recommendations about man-made forms of life, the food we eat, the direction in which multinationals are moving and their aims, how to control what is happening and how to improve the trend of events.

General Introduction

This review is a summary of some relevant information <1> published on the subject recently, to evaluate what is happening and determine the trend of events.

We are here looking at what multinationals are doing with genetic engineering, with biotechnology, with the basic physiological building blocks of plant, animal and human life.

And we are trying to see what is happening and is likely to happen as a result of recent international agreements about private ownership of life-forms. Changed and new life-forms can now be owned by multinational corporations, generation after generation.

This is a situation which threatens human independence and freedom. It is a situation in which the nature of profit-motivated and profit-orientated multinationals threatens human health and survival. {1, 2, 3}

Genetic Engineering, Biotechnology, Creating New Life-forms

It is now possible to change the characteristics of a life-form by transferring selected basic building blocks, genes, from one variety to another, from one species to another.

The source of the genes, of the genetic materials which are used, is either non-human or human.

The new life-forms which are created are sometimes called 'transgenic' and may be plants, animals or geneplasm. The 'genome' is the genetic material of an organism.

As regards foodstuffs, there are those organisms which have themselves been genetically modified, and those which contain genetically modified organisms. There are also those from which the genetically modified organisms, which were used in producing them, have been removed. {14}

The moral and ethical questions raised are of fundamental importance. Should we tinker with the basic building blocks of the planetary environment and of life itself? What are the risks and what may be the consequences to our way of living? Do we as human beings have the right to meddle with a set-up which took so long to produce us, when we have only existed for such a comparatively short time?

Are we risking the survival of humankind at a time of exponentially accelerating scientific and technical knowledge, when our human relationships, basic human rights, social care, human equality, freedom and independence, are so inadequate over much of the planet, leave so much to be desired?

Quite apart from the moral and ethical considerations involved in creating a new life-form, the public health risks are extremely high when tinkering with and changing in the twinkling of an eye, and on a massive scale, life-forms which have taken millions of years to evolve slowly by trial and error and by eliminating inadequate or mistaken change. Unpredictable are the resulting direct and indirect effects on the human being, which is the most complicated organism ever produced and which we do not fully understand.

Human-animal Hybrids

Of great concern is the extent to which human biological material is being taken into private ownership. There have been patent applications for human genes and human cell lines. Human genes have been inserted into animals and there is the prospect of human-animal hybrids. {15}

It seems that human embryos can be cloned. And, if unique or novel in some way, patented, cloned and sold? {15}

It has also been reported that male mice have been modified to produce rat sperm, one species being used to modify another. It seems that this technique could, at least in theory, be used to make another animal produce human sperm. {16}

Quoting from the RAFI Communique {15}
> "It may be possible," writes one commentator, "to patent and to enslave human-animal hybrids who think and feel like humans but who lack constitutional protection ..."

The amount of work being done in related fields seems enormous. What has been and is being done? What are the likely social consequences? Who gains, who loses?

Just what is the underlying purpose of this thrusting ahead into the unknown without serious informed public debate, evaluation and control?

What is needed is independent grassroots <3> evaluation in terms which are meaningful to the community. And public debate and public control of direction, speed and application of all matters relating to human genes, human cell lines and human-animal modifications.

Transgenic Foodstuffs

There are now many transgenic foodstuffs which are being secretly developed, manufactured and produced. We are not being told openly and consistently what is being tried out and for what purpose. Transgenic foodstuffs and foodstuffs which contain transgenic materials are not being labelled as such.

Some Publicly Known Transgenic Organisms

Tomatoes {12, 13}

The flounder has a gene which protects against freezing. This gene has been transferred into a tomato to make freezing of tomatoes possible. Such tomatoes need to be clearly labelled, and this applies to foodstuffs containing them, to show vegetarians that these tomatoes contain an animal component.

Other transgenic tomatoes are being produced and distributed which take about twice the normal time to ripen, apparently to increase the time they can be displayed on shop shelves before going bad. This tomato is resistant to an antibiotic and there are fears that this resistance can be passed on to human beings.

Pigs

It seems that about 50 transgenic pigs were sold for human consumption in Australia. And I have seen a separate report from which it appears that rat genes have been transferred to pigs in an attempt to increase their reproductive capacity.

Salmon

Genetically modified salmon have been produced which apparently grow quickly to something like 40 times their normal weight.

It seems that steps are being taken to farm genetically modified salmon in Scotland and in a South American country.

One would like to see some confirmation that such quick-growing fish are normally developed and shaped. And one would like to know the possible risks involved.

Cows Producing Human Milk Proteins

A human gene has been transferred to a bull to see if next-generation cows produce human milk proteins. {12}

A producer of baby foods and powders pulled out from participating in this development after environmental groups threatened to boycott products of the companies which had invested in the bull.

Wheat {13}

A field of transgenic wheat is being grown in Britain. One of the new genes comes from maize.

Others

Others which also seem to be at a field trial or marketing stage:

> Maize (corn-on-the-cob)
>
> Rennet (used in cheese making)
>
> Rape-seed plant (rape-oil used in foodstuffs, animal feed, cosmetics)

and no doubt many others at the different stages from research and development to field trial and pre-marketing or marketing.

Risks to Public Health

Transferred genes may carry with them the potential to cause allergic reactions. Some people are allergic to nuts. When a Brazil nut gene was transferred to Soya beans, tests showed that those allergic to Brazil nuts were apparently also allergic to the transgenetic Soya beans and it seems that this could have had fatal results.

Also, transferred genes may provide resistance to antibiotics. Considering foodstuffs, there is the risk that such resistance could be transferred to human beings. This is an extremely serious matter from the public health point of view as bacteria already mutate naturally and so develop resistance to antibiotics.

Bacteria are becoming resistant to antibiotics so quickly that we are running out of antibiotics for treating common and fatal diseases. Take tuberculosis. There are now individual cases where only one out of eight or nine antibiotics remains effective. Introducing transgenic foodstuffs into the food-chain may in effect knock out vital antibiotics on which we have come to rely and for which there is no substitute.

We are in the dark about the genome, that is the total genetic material, of plants and animals from which and to which genes are being transferred. What happens to the transgenic organism as a result of transferring genes, and the consequent effects on public health, appear to be unknown and unpredictable.

Now consider that multinationals are large organisations. Large organisations tend to be authoritarian and this means they are relatively inefficient and apply a pretty tough style of management. Mistakes are unlikely to be admitted within the organisation even after customers complain, and the organisation does not readily learn from experience. The same mistakes tend to be made again and again. {9, 10}

It also seems that corporation, industry or government bodies which evaluate such research, development and application, are more concerned with commercial interests and profits than with the needs of the community and effective protection of public life and health.

Hence what is missing is independent public grassroots evaluation of whether new life-forms are needed or desirable.

What is also missing is independent grassroots evaluation of likely effects on human health and on the food-chain at all stages from proposed research to labelling and marketing, by the many independent experts among us. What is being planned, and what is being done, could be and should be discussed openly in specific Internet unmoderated newsgroups. Anonymity would have to be guaranteed to whistle-blowers.

Labelling of Foodstuffs

We seem to be facing an increasing number of transgenic foodstuffs progressing through field trials to the point of marketing to the public without consumers being aware of which foodstuffs are modified, and why they were modified, and likely or possible risks and dangers. We should have the right to know and the right to see clearly at the point of sale what is being sold to us.

Consumers are in this way prevented from making an informed choice, from expressing considered opinions in a practical and effective way by refusing to buy such products. Consumers are thus at present prevented from boycotting potentially harmful products.

Jews and Moslems are concerned about foodstuffs which contain genes from animals which their religion forbids them to eat. Vegetarians have to know which transgenic plants contain animal genes.

As far as I know, the Co-operative Wholesale Society is the UK's only major UK supermarket which has declared its intention to label all genetically altered foodstuffs and has started to do so.

Plant Breeding and Plant Gene Banks. Providing and Marketing of Plants, Animals and Seeds.

Multinational corporations which supply agrochemicals (fertilisers, pesticides and herbicides) have been allowed to buy up all well-known seed providers of any appreciable size. Commercial plant breeding would seem to be in the hands of multinational corporations who now control all the significant plant gene banks. {7, 12}

Such a multinational is likely to try to develop plants which respond well to the other agrochemicals it markets.

Indeed, 'the world's chief crops have been scientifically studied to see how they can be genetically adapted to ensure a monopoly control over their cultivation, harvesting, production and distribution.' {12}

A hybrid plant does not produce usable seeds and farmers growing it have to buy new seed every year.

As a rule, farmers keep back some of their crop to use as seed in the following year. But if a gene from another plant could induce sterility {12} in the plant he is cropping, then the farmer would have to buy new seeds each year and he (and thus we) could become dependent for our existence on a few large organisations. On organisations which aim to maximise their private profits and which appear to be only inadequately held to account for the social consequences of their actions.

Hence it would seem essential to obtain reliable information about the purpose of particular transgenic modifications.

And also about research and developments which could harm the community, in this and related areas.

Patenting New Life-forms. GATT.

'Ownership' has been defined as 'the right to possess an item of property' and so one has to ask where the right comes from and how it is exercised.

The term 'intellectual property rights' has been used in connection with the patenting of new life-forms. Such a patent provides the holder of the patent with the recognised ownership of the new life-form. So it would seem that ownership rights over new life-forms are based on man-made laws and that there has been little, if any, grassroots participation in their drafting.

There is a United Nations treaty on global biodiversity. Some financial return must be paid to the country of origin if a company wishes legally to exploit the country's natural resources. However, it seems that only a few drugs companies have started to make payments to some research institutes or governments while no benefits are being returned to indigenous forest communities.

The GATT agreement (General Agreement on Tariffs and Trade) is a treaty between many countries which aims to free international trade and reduce tariffs. In this way it serves the interests of multinationals at the expense of the economic and social interests and welfare of individual countries.

GATT also aims to give exclusive protection to patent holders for 20 years. Patent holders may demand royalty payments on their inventions. Strict enforcement criteria are imposed. 'Astonishingly, the rules place the onus of proof in case of dispute on the farmers, a provision going against normal rules of justice' {8}. The resulting costs could prevent the vast mass of small farmers from disputing the source of the seeds they are using.

Patenting can and is now used to prevent living organisms being copied. GATT also requires a country to protect patents owned by foreigners. Third world peasant farmers go unrewarded while huge royalty payments will have to be made to multinational corporations.

And as royalty payments can be collected from patented seeds, multinationals are likely to market these in preference to older and established varieties.

Traditional Agriculture, Farming Products and Native Knowledge. Rights of Indigenous People.

Farmers keep back each year some of their crop to use as seed in the following year. In the course of centuries farmers' decisions about what to grow under their particular circumstances, and how to grow it, amounted to a natural and cumulative process of selection for yield, flavour and resistance to environmental hazards.

In the same way local people in India, Africa, Amazonian rain forests, the Philippines and elsewhere, have much traditional knowledge about local plant and animal life. This knowledge of domestic and commercial uses, and medicinal properties, has been handed down and enlarged, generation by generation, and is the property of the local indigenous people.

'The overwhelming bulk of the genetic raw materials used in the laboratories of western companies are derived from farms and forests in the developing countries' {4}. 'What is happening is that genetic material from anywhere is being patented, mainly in the US and resulting seed marketed; this means that farmers will have lost their rights to their own original stocks, and not be allowed under Gatt to market or use them' {6}.

'About a quarter of the world's pharmaceutical products, including anaesthetics, anti-leukaemia drugs and contraceptives, owe their origins to wild plants. And the 1990s have seen a resurgence of interest in natural sources. More than 100 research institutes and 70 companies worldwide are now actively investigating the healing potential of plants used for centuries by indigenous peoples.' {11}

It seems that in recent years local and multinational companies 'have all plundered the knowledge of indigenous people'. The Intellectual Property Rights of indigenous people need protecting 'with regard to the plants they have developed over the centuries' and 'there should be compensation for this stolen knowledge'. {7, 11}

Worldwide Farming

Non-hybrid seeds can be replanted and farmers traditionally save part of one year's crop to use as seed for planting in the following year.

Farmers buying patented seeds and then saving some of their crop for resowing, will have to pay royalties each year to the patent-holder. And apparently royalties would have to be paid for patented animals in the same way.

These patented seeds are likely to depend on agrochemicals produced by the same multinational which produced the seeds, with farmers then becoming dependent on one supplier for seed, fertilisers, herbicides and pesticides.

Resulting in enormous profits to the patent holders, that is to multinationals, and doubtless these companies have the muscle to enforce their demands.

'The freedom of farmers worldwide is lost and they all become dependant and trapped by a few large companies.' {6}

Hybrid seeds, however, cannot be resown. Such seeds have to be repurchased each year. It would seem that multinationals are working on genetic modifications aimed at converting non-hybrid plants such as wheat into hybrids which would compel farmers to repurchase seed from the multinational each year.

Farmers, and thus the community as a whole, could then be dependent for plant and animal foodstuffs on a few large, profit-motivated and profit-orientated multinational corporations.

Farming in Low-wage (Third-world, Underdeveloped) Countries

Small farmers will now be unable to save seeds from their crops for replanting at no extra cost the following year, as they have done for many generations. They will either have to pay royalties for patented seeds to a multinational or else buy new seeds each year.

Seed companies intend to enforce this {5}. It has been estimated that the US will gain $61 billion a year from Third World royalties.

As a consequence, many millions of poor peasants and farmers are likely to be shifted off the land into city slums because they cannot afford to purchase and annually repurchase seeds or the agrochemical inputs (fertilisers, pesticides) required by new plant seeds. {8}

Reactions to GATT

In India, 500,000 farmers marched in protest against the GATT proposals and adopted these resolutions {6}:

- To oppose the entry of multinational corporations
- To establish Community Intellectual Property Rights for Third World Farmers over their biowealth
- To establish an International Farmer-Scientist Co-operative Research Institute
- To continue the free exchange of seeds and biowealth between Third World farmers
- To confirm that food security is sacrosanct and all countries should be free to formulate their own agricultural policies
- To put the burden of proving the source of their patented seed on multinational corporations

Protests intensified as the signing of the GATT approached. To many small farmers of the Third World it was clear that their survival was threatened by its provisions.

Here and there some Third World farmers are reacting:

- Some farmers plan to produce their own hybrids.
- One union's research centre has started to grow native seeds for storage, development and distribution.

Conclusions

Multinationals

Changed and new life-forms can now be owned by multinational corporations, generation after generation. This is a situation in which the nature of profit-motivated and profit-orientated multinationals threatens human independence and freedom, human health and survival.

Of great concern is the extent to which human biological material is being taken into private ownership. And, thinking ahead, we need to consider the prospect of human clones and human-animal hybrids being taken into private multinational ownership.

There are now many transgenic foodstuffs which are being secretly developed, manufactured and produced. An increasing number of transgenic foodstuffs are progressing through field trials to the point of marketing to the public.

But transgenic foodstuffs, and foodstuffs which contain transgenic materials, are not being labelled as such. So consumers are not being told which of the foodstuffs they are buying have been modified, and why they were modified.

This prevents consumers from voting with their purses, from expressing considered opinions in a practical and effective way by refusing to buy such products, from boycotting potentially harmful products.

Multinational corporations which supply agrochemicals have been allowed to buy up all well-known seed providers of any appreciable size. Commercial plant breeding would seem to be in the hands of multinational corporations who now control all the significant plant gene banks. {7, 12}

Hence a few multinationals have apparently established what amounts to a stranglehold, a form of monopoly control, over an essential step in the planet-wide supply of foodstuffs.

GATT (General Agreement on Tariffs and Trade) is a treaty between many countries which aims to free international trade and reduce tariffs. In this way it serves the interests of multinationals at the expense of the economic and social interests and welfare of individual countries.

The GATT agreement apparently gives exclusive protection to patent holders for 20 years and imposes strict enforcement criteria. Huge royalty payments will have to be made to multinational corporations. 'Astonishingly, the rules place the onus of proof in case of dispute on the farmers, a provision going against normal rules of justice' {8}. The resulting costs could prevent the vast mass of small farmers from disputing the source of the seeds they are using.

'Ownership' has been defined as 'the right to possess an item of property' and so one has to ask where the right comes from and how it is exercised. It would seem that ownership rights over new life-forms are based on man-made laws and that there has been little, if any, grassroots community-orientated participation in their drafting.

'The overwhelming bulk of the genetic raw materials used in the laboratories of western companies are derived from farms and forests in the developing countries' {4}. 'What is happening is that genetic material from anywhere is being patented, mainly in the US and resulting seed marketed. {6}.

Farmers buying patented seeds and then saving some of their crop for resowing, will have to pay royalties each year to the patent-holder. And apparently royalties would have to be paid for patented animals in the same way.

These patented seeds are likely to depend on agrochemicals produced by the same multinational which produced the seeds, with farmers then becoming dependent on one supplier for seed, fertilisers, herbicides and pesticides.

Resulting in enormous profits to the patent holders, that is to multinationals, and doubtless these companies have the muscle to enforce their demands.

Many millions of poor peasants and small farmers are likely to be shifted off the land into city slums because they cannot afford to purchase and annually repurchase seeds or the agrochemical inputs (fertilisers, pesticides) required by new plant seeds {8}.

All farmers worldwide, and thus the community as a whole, could become dependent for plant and animal foodstuffs on a few large, profit-motivated and profit-orientated multinational corporations. This would place these corporations, their owners and directors, in a position of extraordinary power over people.

So it seems that we are expected to buy genetically modified foodstuffs without questioning what we are getting or what the risks are. It also looks as if large multinationals are attempting to establish a stranglehold, a form of monopoly control, over an essential step in the planet-wide supply of foodstuffs, namely the production and marketing of seeds. And that they have been given ownership over new life-forms and the power to force farmers worldwide to pay the multinational each year for seeds even when these seeds were grown by the farmer the previous year.

When there are only a few large multinationals sharing a market, then at this sort of scale they may well not be competing with each other effectively. And so it looks as if the world population is in danger of being exploited by multinationals who would be in a position of extraordinary power over people.

Community

Plants and animals are being modified to obtain new life-forms. The moral and ethical questions raised are of fundamental importance and need public discussion and debate.

What happens to the transgenic organism as a result of transferring genes, and the consequent effects on public health, appear to be unknown and unpredictable. The effects on human beings are unpredictable. The public health risks are extremely high.

What is known is that transferred genes may carry with them the potential to cause allergic reactions and may provide resistance to antibiotics.

Bacteria are becoming resistant to antibiotics so quickly that we are running out of antibiotics for treating common and fatal diseases. Introducing transgenic foodstuffs into the food-chain may in effect knock out vital antibiotics on which we have come to rely and for which there is no substitute.

This is a serious matter from a public health point of view.

We are not being told openly and consistently what is being tried out and for what purpose.

For example, there are now many transgenic foodstuffs which are being secretly developed, manufactured and produced. An increasing number of transgenic foodstuffs are progressing through field trials to the point of marketing to the public.

But transgenic foodstuffs, and foodstuffs which contain transgenic materials, are not being labelled as such. So consumers are not being told which of the foodstuffs they are buying have been modified, and why they were modified.

This prevents consumers from voting with their purses, from expressing considered opinions in a practical and effective way by refusing to buy such products, from boycotting potentially harmful products.

Of great concern is the extent to which human biological material is being taken into private ownership. There have been patent applications for human genes and human cell lines. Human genes have been inserted into animals and there is the prospect of human-animal hybrids. {15}

The amount of work being done in related fields seems enormous. What has been and is being done? What are the likely social consequences? Who gains, who loses? Just what is the underlying purpose of this thrusting ahead into the unknown without serious informed public debate, evaluation and control?

What is needed is independent grassroots <3> evaluation in terms which are meaningful to the community. And public debate and public control of direction, speed and application of all matters relating to human genes, human cell lines and human-animal modifications.

Recommendations

Multinationals

1. Traditional plant and animal varieties need to be collected and propagated, country by country. And this needs to be done quickly and effectively.

    Far-seeing individuals and groups have already started, one example being the Irish Seed Savers Association.

    Such collections need to belong to the community. This means that each collection has to be run and controlled as a co-operative under rules which prevent it being taken over or dissolved by private interests, and that it has to be supported by ample public funds.

    Collections already being formed should be amply supported from public funds on the basis that they will be freely available.

2. Collection, storage, propagation and distribution of seeds and animals needs to be nationalised, country by country, placing them under public ownership.

    The key objective of such enterprises should be service to the community.

    In this case the aims of nationalising are

    (a) to prevent multinationals from gaining a monopoly-like stranglehold on this essential stage in food production,

    (b) to regain control of food production from multinationals and place it again in the hands of the elected representatives of the people.

    (c) And to ensure that a country's food production remains under the control of its elected representatives.

3. It is essential to raise public awareness of all the issues involved, such as

    3.1 Of all the issues involved in creating, patenting, owning, selling and using new life-forms of any kind or shape.

    3.2 Whenever international agreements and national or international legislation favour the operations of multinationals instead of serving local communities or people in general.

3.3 Whenever corporate takeovers or mergers are against the national interest of any nation.

3.4 Of the need for the right to know about, and to comment on, and participate in, all aspects of government and corporate decision taking.

4. To concentrate agriculture and farming on traditional varieties grown organically combined with 'organic' animal farming.

    Particularly so since "reliance on inputs of inorganic fertiliser and pesticide was not sustainable ecologically or economically, due to rising costs, falling yields, soil deterioration and resistance to insecticides." {8}

5. Publicly owned and funded but co-operatively directed and managed farming research institutes.

    They need to belong to the community as their main objective should be to serve the community and not any kind of private interests, and they should be supported by ample public funds.

    They have to be run and controlled as co-operatives under rules which prevent them being taken over or dissolved by private interests.

    It may be that genetic modifications of plants or animals should only be researched and carried out in such institutions, to ensure that public service, which is service to the community, takes precedence over, and is more important than, profit motivation and private profit, wealth and power over other people.

6. Ensure that no multinational misuses its power to obtain a determining or controlling interest, share or hold on its market.

7. To enforce existing anti-trust and anti-monopoly legislation nationally and internationally.

    And to install such legislation where it does not exist already.

8. We need to develop co-operative employee and customer owned co-operatives founded in such a way that they cannot be taken over by, or sold to, or divided or dispersed to become, profit-motivated entities. Neither must its own directors or management be able to change the co-operative service-orientated purpose of the co-operative enterprise towards profit-orientation.

9. We need also to consider the prospect and implications of human cloning and human-animal hybridisation, and the implications of new life-forms being legally assigned to 'owners', to profit orientated multinational corporations.

Community

What is needed is independent grassroots evaluation of such dangerous research and developments, at all stages from planning to application, in terms which are meaningful to the community.

Human-animal Hybrids

What is missing is independent public grassroots evaluation of whether such new life-forms are needed or desirable.

What is needed here is serious informed public debate and public control of direction, speed and application of all matters relating to human genes, human cell lines and human-animal modifications.

For example, we need to consider the prospect of human clones and human-animal hybrids being taken into private multinational ownership.

Providing and Marketing of Plants, Animals and Seeds

What is missing is independent public grassroots evaluation of whether such new life-forms are needed or desirable.

It seems essential to obtain reliable information about the purpose of particular transgenic modifications.

Risks to Public Health

What is missing here is independent grassroots evaluation of likely effects on human health and on the food-chain at all stages from proposed research to labelling and marketing, by the many independent experts among us.

What is being planned, and what is being done, could be and should be discussed openly, possibly in specific Internet unmoderated newsgroups. Anonymity would have to be guaranteed to whistle-blowers.

Labelling of Foodstuffs

Transgenic foodstuffs and foodstuffs which contain transgenic materials are not being labelled as such.

We should have the right to know and the right to see clearly at the point of sale what is being sold to us.

Consumers have to be able to make informed choices, to vote with their purses, to express considered opinions in a practical and effective way by refusing to buy undesirable products, to boycott potentially harmful products.

The Rights of Indigenous People

The Intellectual Property Rights of indigenous people need protecting 'with regard to the plants they have developed over the centuries' and they should be compensated when this is taken from them and used by others.

Notes and References

Notes

<1> For further information see {4-8, 11-14}

<2> 'Socially irresponsible' meaning that they are not being adequately held to account for the social consequences of what they are doing.

<3> 'Grassroots' meaning the basic or fundamental level of ordinary people, informed, independent, community orientated.

References

{ 1} Social Responsibility, Profits and Social Accountability.
Incidents, Disasters and Catastrophes.
The Worldwide Struggle for Social Accountability.
Community Aims and Community Leadership.
Manfred Davidmann, 1979, 1995
solhaam.org

{ 2} In 'Management and Leadership:
      Local, National, Multinational (Global),
      Principles and Practice'
      Manfred Davidmann
      ISBN 978-0-85192-057-3
      See chapter 4: 'Motivation'

{ 3} See chapter 16:
      'The Will to Work: What People Struggle to Achieve'
      Manfred Davidmann

{ 4} Battle for the Rights of Life. Who Owns Life?
      Kevin Watkins
      Guardian 17/07/92

{ 5} Seeds of Discontent
      John Vidal
      Guardian 01/10/93

{ 6} Freedom of Farmers Lost
      Dr Ulrich E Loening
      Guardian 30/11/93

{ 7} Sowing Seeds of Dissent
      John Herbert
      Guardian 05/03/94

{ 8} Seeds of Discontent
      Walter Schwarz
      Guardian 11/03/94

{ 9} In 'Management and Leadership:
      Local, National, Multinational (Global),
      Principles and Practice'
      Manfred Davidmann
      ISBN 978-0-85192-057-3
      See chapter 2: 'Style of Management and
      Leadership'

{10} In 'Management and Leadership:
      Local, National, Multinational (Global),
      Principles and Practice'
      Manfred Davidmann
      ISBN 978-0-85192-057-3
      See chapter 3: 'Role of Managers under Different
      Styles of Management'

{11} Intellectual Property Rights to Rainforest Products
      Polly Ghazi
      Observer 10/07/94

96

{12}   Designer Genes
       Colin Spencer
       Guardian 24/09/94

{13}   Fried Gene Tomatoes
       Polly Ghazi,
       Observer 25/09/94

{14}   Gentechnik im Nahrungsmittelbereich:
       Kennzeichnungspflicht wird definiert.
       Dr. Stephan Mertens
       Deutsches Aerzteblatt, 93, No.18, 03/05/96, 29.

{15}   The Patenting of Human Genetic Material
       RAFI Communique Jan/Feb 1994
       Rural Advancement Foundation International

{16}   Animal-human Sperm 'Possible'
       Tim Radford
       Guardian 30/05/96

Chapter 10

What People are Struggling Against: How Society is Organised for Controlling and Exploiting People

Summary
Motivation of Top-level Leadership
Decision-making in Companies
Social System
Ownership and Control of Moneys (Capital, Savings, Wealth)
    Capital Taken from Customers
    Ownership
    Taking Possession of the Population's Savings
    Ownership and Control
Government Activities
    Transferring Taxpayers' Moneys to Enterprises
    Condoning Tax Avoidance by Enterprises
    Using Taxpayers' Moneys to Pay Operating Costs of Enterprises
    Condoning Tax Avoidance by the Rich
    Taxing the Working Population More Severely
    Serving Enterprises and the Rich
Profit Maximising
Corrupted Economics
Misleading Experts
Authoritarian Struggle to take over and Control Decision-making by Transferring it to Leaders
    Top-level Leadership Taking Over Decision-making in Business, Service and Community Organisations
    Top-level Leadership Taking Over Decision-making from the Population
        Participative Organisation: The Meaning of 'Democracy'
        Decision-making and Policy-setting within Political Party and by Government
        Selecting and Electing Representatives: 'Closed-list' System of Proportional Representation

Summary

This main report brings together key conclusions from four studies {1-4}
undertaken to obtain a better understanding of why people have to
struggle throughout their adult lives, in all countries and organisations,
at all levels, to maintain and improve their standard of living and quality
of life. We know what people are struggling to achieve {13, 14} and so
this study was undertaken to explore why people have to struggle by
looking at what they are struggling against.

The report looks at the way 'Economics' has been used to misinform and
mislead the general public, and looks at the role and vested interests of
experts. It describes how companies (corporations) accumulate their
capital and reserves from moneys taken from customers and how
people's massive savings are placed under the control of others. And
shows how taxpayers' moneys are used in different ways to enlarge the
profits of companies.

It discusses and illustrates the internal struggles taking place in political parties and all other organisations, for achieving greater democracy and against those wishing to overpower democratic processes of decision-taking.

Motivation of Top-level Leadership {2}

Directors are motivated by pay in its various forms, by greater wealth and by greater influence which includes dispensing patronage, and by power. The pay of directors is what owners decide to pay themselves and their directors, and increases with increasing influence and power.

Considering mergers and take-overs, we see top-level leaderships battling with each other for more power, for greater control, over people and resources.

Decision-making in Companies {2}

Owners take the profits but have transferred much of their own risk to other people, to suppliers, customers, and employees, by limiting their liability for the debts of their companies.

The person who is the majority shareholder in effect controls the company <1> and decides what is to be done and how it is to be done. So the system is organised so that a few, a relatively very few, people at the top take the key decisions.

Although a company does not take decisions it can be held responsible and can be held to account for decisions taken by individuals within it. To that extent it serves as a front behind which those who take key decisions can hide, as a front for owners and directors.

The most effective control of corporate irresponsibility appears to be the fear of bad publicity, of public awareness of socially irresponsible company behaviour, with its effect on company image, consumer trust and market share, and thus on profits. Particularly so when publicity names those responsible for making antisocial decisions within the company, and those responsible for condoning, or for omitting to restrain, the company's antisocial activities. {1}

Social System

We see a pattern of differentials which rewards service to the owners and their establishment rather than ability or service to the community. The pay of directors is what owners decide to pay themselves. Nurses, teachers, fire-fighters and police officers are at present paid comparatively little for the work they do. {2}

Ownership and Control of Moneys (Capital, Savings, Wealth)

Capital Taken from Customers {2}

Customers are not given a choice. Enterprises (their owners) simply take their customers' moneys

> for getting back money already spent on the business and

> for expanding the business without giving the community corresponding ownership rights.

Enterprises <1> collect moneys from their customers by the simple expedient of charging more than their actual costs.

The source of profit (surplus) is thus money collected from their customers, is money which belongs to customers.

When one buys goods or services, the price includes not only the manufacturer's and supplier's costs and profits, but also includes moneys (depreciation; capital replacement) for replacing their buildings and equipment. So an enterprise collects from its customers whatever its assets like equipment and buildings have cost, doing so without paying income tax on the amounts it collects.

And enterprises (their owners) are also continually collecting money from their customers and are enriching themselves by adding these moneys to their reserves.

Shareholders would not even consider handing their moneys over to a company without in return becoming an owner of a corresponding part of the company, without getting a corresponding number of shares in return. But all these moneys are taken by enterprises (their owners) without in return giving corresponding ownership rights to their customers or the community.

Even co-operatives and mutual aid societies (building societies, credit unions) have been retaining some of their members' profits each year, for no apparent valid reason, accumulating these moneys for over 150 years <4>. By continually adding these moneys to their reserves they have become rich and powerful. Their chief executives and directors have become powerful, influential, and well paid.

Ownership {2}

Ownership laws which assign ownership 'rights' to owners have been devised by the owners themselves or by those who serve them. Ownership of land and means of production, of funds and wealth, has always been accumulated at someone else's expense. All belonged to the community, belonged to all alike.

To 'rob' is to take unlawfully. But we are here looking at moneys being taken legally and largely without the customer's (owner's) informed knowledge or agreement. What is taking place is perhaps best described by the phrase 'legalised robbery'.

Taking Possession of the Population's Savings {2}

Company pension funds run into many GBP billions and between them own, and thus are in position to influence and control, much if not most of UK's share capital. Including company credit unions and providers of private pensions, such moneys and funds should be under the control of those who contributed and those who are contributing to them. But ultimate control, and the power and influence that goes with it, have in effect been taken from the working population and placed in the hands of those who own and control companies (corporations).

Instead of being under the control of those who contributed, these moneys are in effect placed under the control of a few people at the top who in this way gain power, are enabled to dispense patronage (and support each other), gain high incomes and much wealth.

Ownership and Control {2}

What we see is a system where owners and top-level leaderships enrich themselves by taking or using and risking other people's moneys.

This 'legalised robbery' seems to be a key feature of the way society is organised to benefit those at the top.

Government Activities

Government activities serve business enterprises (owners) by

> Transferring taxpayers' moneys to enterprises.

> Condoning tax avoidance by enterprises (making good the loss by collecting more taxes from the population).

> Using taxpayers' moneys to pay operating costs of enterprises.

And serve business enterprises and the rich by

> Condoning tax avoidance by the rich.

> Taxing the working population more severely.

Transferring Taxpayers' Moneys to Enterprises {3}

Some employers pay wages which are so low that employees are forced to work long hours merely to survive. A government may then make up such wages with means-tested income support benefits to a poverty-existence level. Which is apparently what happened in the UK while minimum-wage requirements ceased to be applied. In such ways taxpayers' moneys are used to subsidise the profits of companies, of their owners.

Taxpayers' moneys are also used to subsidise the profits of companies when a government pays a subsidy to a company for every new employee. This is so regardless of whether the subsidy is paid as a single payment or whether it is paid for a limited period as part of the employee's wage.

Overall, the amounts channelled similarly into private profits seem large. There may be investment grants, depreciation allowances, grants in aid, tax allowances, tax-free benefits, loans at favourable terms or other ways of financial support to enterprises in industry, agriculture and the service sector.

Very large amounts are apparently handed over yearly in such ways to increase the wealth and power of a small number of people without any corresponding return to the community. They are generally given without a corresponding transfer of ownership rights and control to those who provided the money, to the community.

Condoning Tax Avoidance by Enterprises (making good the loss by collecting more taxes from the population) {3}

A multinational company can minimise its liability for corporation tax by transfer pricing, that is by making book entries which transfer profits to the country with the lowest corporation tax {5}. This tax avoidance is legal and governments have not legislated to prevent this practice.

So citizens pay more tax, the government can now spend the same amount as before, the multinational's profits have increased. In other words, the multinational's increased profits arise from moneys which are in effect collected by the government from its taxpayers.

The multinational, and this means the owners and directors of the multinational, are thus in effect taxing the people and in this way increasing the multinational's profits and thus the incomes and wealth of its owners and directors.

A unitary taxation system can overcome this tax avoidance by assessing the actual profits being generated by a multinational in a particular country. American state governments have tried to install systems of unitary taxation but, as far as I know, multinational corporations have been able to dissuade state governments from applying such systems.

Using Taxpayers' Moneys to Pay Operating Costs of Enterprises {3}

The mark-up between buying or producing in a low-wage country, and then selling in a high-wage country, is often enormous <5>. Large additional profits result. Unemployment increases in the home country. There are many costs associated with unemployment such as social security payments to the newly unemployed.

It is accepted as a principle of economics that social costs have to be paid by those causing them, a well-known example being the social costs arising from polluting. So the social costs of unemployment have to be paid by the enterprise which caused the unemployment in the first place.

Companies, however, are not made to pay the resulting costs of unemployment, are allowed to pass these operating costs to the community and are thus making large profits at the expense of the community.

Not having to pay the resulting social costs of unemployment, companies can readily and socially-irresponsibly reduce wages and thus the standard of living in a country by threatening to move their production facilities to another country.

They do so for the sake of private profit but no action is taken to prevent them from doing so by recovering the social costs from them, or to deter and punish such socially-irresponsible activities by punitive penalties.

Condoning Tax Avoidance by the Rich {3}

There would seem to be no good or valid reason for condoning tax-avoidance by those who are rich.

What stands out is that there are ways in which the rich can avoid paying their share of the tax load. By placing their funds in offshore and tax-free locations or by locating companies elsewhere, to give just two examples.

Condoning tax-avoidance by the rich increases the tax load on the working population.

Taxing the Working Population More Severely {3}

The government spends for the community the money it receives from the community, collecting it through taxation.

When owner-serving governments 'reduce income tax' for individuals and companies, it is the rich who gain much, the working population hardly benefits. One then sees that the amounts contributed by the rich are being drastically reduced.

To claim in such circumstances that government expenditure on public services has to be cut so as to make ends meet, appears to be a one-sided viewpoint.

Moneys saved by spending less on social security for those in need and gained by collecting more tax from the working population, are apparently being used to reduce the taxes collected from the rich and from companies.

Serving Enterprises and the Rich {3}

So what we have seen is that taxpayers' moneys are used in different ways to enlarge the profits of companies and thus of their owners, and to make the rich even richer.

We saw that companies are in effect allowed to tax the population and are also allowed to pass large parts of their operating costs to the taxpayers.

And that tax avoidance by enterprises and by the rich is condoned, the government making good the resulting loss by collecting more taxes from the working population.

Moneys saved by spending less on social security for those in need and moneys gained by collecting more tax from the working population, are apparently being used to reduce the taxes collected from the rich and from companies.

And when taxing the working population more severely, the ways in which taxation can be used to shift the tax load between income groups are numerous and often hide behind fine-sounding phrases.

Profit Maximising

In practice directors are generally required by owner-serving laws to act first and foremost in the interests of the owners, so that it is profit which is maximised. Short-term and long-term profits can be and are being maximised. {1}

When profit becomes an overriding or sole objective to owners, directors or managers, they concentrate on maximising profits regardless of cost to others. Profits are then maximised regardless of the cost and consequences to the community, limited only by the likelihood of unpleasant consequences such as restraining fines, punitive legal punishment or adverse publicity. {1, 2}

One of the requirements for the free-market economic system to work, is that profit margins and prices need to be controlled effectively so as to protect the community from exploitation. But they are not. {2}

To owners and employers the worth of a job is what has to be paid to get it done. They want work to be done at the lowest rate at which they can get it done as profits can be increased by reducing labour costs, by exploiting employees.

Owners and employers use inflation as an excuse for reducing real wages and salaries of the working population so as to increase profits. Employees are then not compensated for increased skill, experience and responsibility, do not receive their share of the increasing national income and wealth. UK pensions have now to be increased by 34 percent just to reach the level at which they should be now. And pensioners still have to be compensated for the moneys withheld from them without good reason by the government since 1980. This attack on the living standards of the working population is misleadingly called a 'fight (or battle) against inflation' to persuade the working population to tighten its belts, to reduce its standard of living, so as to increase profits. {1}

So owners and employers will, when they can, pressurise the working population into accepting even lower rates of pay by increasing the working population's needs. Doing so by advocating greater unemployment, reducing social security, reducing national health service provisions, weakening the quality of education (knowledge, clear thinking, understanding, objective evaluation). {1}

And, as said already, moneys saved by government by spending less on social security for those in need and moneys gained by collecting more tax from the working population, are apparently being used by owner-serving governments to reduce the taxes collected from the rich and from companies. {3}

In addition, purchasing power is being transferred from the bottom to the top. It has been estimated that 10 percent of the UK population were sinking into direct poverty, any gains in income being overtaken by the increasing cost of living. The next 20 percent were losing out, were being reduced to relative poverty. On the other hand the top 0.4 percent of the population took gains in take-home purchasing power which were 100 times those received by the general population. This was the situation some time ago but it seems to have got worse rather than better. {2}

More or less ignored is the large top-level remuneration which has been increasing yearly for some years at up to four or five times the rate of inflation, increasing each year by amounts many times exceeding the average income of the working population. {1}

So profits are apparently being maximised regardless of the cost to others, to the community. Without care or concern for the condition, standard of living or quality of life of the working population. Without being concerned about the in sum-total enormous human suffering which results. {1}

Overall, what we see are consequences of decisions made at the top, and the results of putting them into effect. Results and consequences which at times make the decisions seem so brutal that they appear inhuman. {1}

Corrupted Economics {1}

Misleading biased interpretations and pronouncements are made in the name of 'economics' which relate to exploiting people at work, as citizens, and in the market place. It appears that misleading and inappropriate terms are used which confuse instead of illuminate, and which seem intended to confuse.

Index-linking is an accepted way of taking the heat out of employer and employee pay bargaining. After index linking, pay bargaining can concentrate on the main issue, namely on how to share out the increased value created by the joint effort of both sides, and on how to adjust national differentials to ensure that no one section gains unfairly at the expense of others and to balance out inequalities.

A ruling establishment could be expected to avoid and resist index-linking of pay because index-linking would limit their efforts to increase profits by lowering the standard of living of the working population.

But what stands out is the way the UK's trade union and Labour party establishments appear to have neglected index-linking for so many years.

Misleading Experts {1}

An expert is supposed to advise to the best of his ability, knowledge, skill and experience and is responsible, that is accountable, for the quality of his advice. Responsible, that is accountable, also to those he is advising.

Too often do experts tell people what the expert thinks is good for the people to do. Too often it is the expert who decides or who attempts to compel others to do as told.

Employers have a strong influence on what their employees say in public and employees are likely to be advocating viewpoints which are employer-serving instead of being people-serving and community-serving.

And bias can be increased even further when media present mainly one point of view, say that of employers, or of a particular political party, or of advertisers.

Authoritarian Struggle to take over and Control Decision-making by Transferring it to Leaders {4}

The report 'Democracy Under Attack: Top-level Leadership and Decision-taking' {4} discusses and illustrates the internal struggles taking place in companies, political parties and other organisations, for achieving greater democracy and against those wishing to overpower democratic processes of decision-taking.

Top-level Leadership Taking Over Decision-making in Business, Service and Community Organisations

We are here looking at decision-making in the management and control of companies, enterprises and all types of community organisations. Looking at the ways in which authoritarian minds attempt to take over and place democratically controlled organisations under authoritarian control.

The confrontation between on the one hand elected policy-making bodies, and on the other hand those who are supposed to put their policies into effect, can be seen in many areas. The abovementioned report {4} shows how the struggle manifests itself under these headings:

> Majority Shareholder Taking Over Decision-taking from Other Shareholders
>
> Trade Union General Secretary or Leader of Political Party Changing the Rules to Increase Personal Power
>
> Reorganising the National Health Service: Replacing Grassroots Decision-taking with Top-level Direction and Control of Spending
>
> Controlling the Use of Capital: User-owned User-benefiting Bank Converted to Profit-motivated Shareholder-benefiting Ownership
>
> Senior Executives Taking Over from Owners: Co-operatives
>
> Senior Executives Taking Over from Owners: Companies
>
> Employee Participation in Decision-making

We can see the struggle in all organisations and at all levels. It is a struggle against authoritarian management or government for the right to take decisions. And in all democratic organisations it is a struggle against the authoritarian mind taking over the decision-taking.

A continuous battle is taking place between on the one hand policy-deciding by the many through elected assemblies, and on the other hand policy-deciding at the top, by a few. This is clearly shown by the way in which full-time officials and executives attempt to take power away from their policy-setting assemblies, after which they attempt to impose their will on the membership or population.

Top-level Leadership Taking Over Decision-making from the Population

Participative Organisation: The Meaning of 'Democracy' <2>

Participative (democratic) organisation {4} rests on the population electing representatives, on the basis of each person having one vote. Representatives are responsible to, and accountable to, the population for putting into effect policies decided by the population.

What underlies participative organisation (democracy) is decision-taking by the people at the level of the people.

And representatives, governments or government officials do not have the authority or right to reduce or sign away the participative (democratic) rights of the electors, of the population.

What needs to be stressed is that in a participative (democratic) organisation policies are decided by a well-informed population at the level of the population and that policies then become binding on management or government. <3>

In an authoritarian organisation the policy decisions are taken at the top or near the top by the hierarchy (establishment) and are binding on the organisation's members. Decision-taking at the top is sometimes referred to as 'deciding centrally'. Authoritarian organisation is the opposite of democracy and underlies dictatorship.

And what we see is conflict between authoritarian minds wishing to dominate, control and exploit on the one hand and, on the other hand, citizens wishing to maintain and improve the standard of living and quality of life for the population as a whole by democratic (grassroots level) decision-taking.

So the real struggle is not between political left and right, but is a struggle for participation (the right to take decisions).

Decision-making and Policy-setting within Political Party and by Government

We are looking at recent and ongoing events {4} and it is difficult to separate facts from opinions. However, an overall pattern emerges which appears to reinforce and strengthen what is said here about top-level leadership attempting to take over decision-taking from the grassroots population, about the consequent struggle in all organisations and at all levels.

The UKs Labour party's annual conference took binding decisions on policy proposals brought up by grassroots membership. They decided policy which the executive had to follow and put into effect.

Under a new party leadership some fundamental changes were introduced and by 1998 the party's annual conference had ceased to decide policies, had ceased to decide what had to be done. Instead of deciding mandatory policies based on direct policy proposals from local branches, the annual conference became a talking-shop, discussing and expressing views on subjects selected and approved by the leadership.

In September 1998 an opinion poll reported that the majority of people felt that the leader of the Labour government was closer to big business than to ordinary people.

Selecting and Electing Representatives: 'Closed-list' System of Proportional Representation {4}

With this system it is not really the electorate which decides whether one is elected as a local representative. Whether one is elected depends on whether one is placed on the list and on one's top-to-bottom position on the list. So whether one is elected depends on the party leader or leadership.

So one's chance of being elected depends on doing as told by leader or leadership, on supporting their policies, instead of depending on serving one's constituents (local electors), instead of being responsible and accountable to the electors, to the community one is supposed to represent and act for.

The higher up one's name appears on the list, the more likely is one to be elected, the more likely is it that one benefits from the high salary, excellent allowances, good working conditions and good pension rights which go with the job. Loyalty to leader or leadership replaces loyalty to electors.

It is the grassroots membership which should select and decide who is to represent them. The party leadership seems to be close to taking over both functions.

What we see taking place with a closed-list system is far removed from being responsible and accountable to one's local electors, to the local community, for the way in which one represents them and looks after their interests both at local and national level. Democratic decision-taking is reversed by a system of closed-list proportional representation as decision-taking by representatives is replaced with obedience to dictates from the top.

Selecting and Electing Representatives: UK Members of European Parliament (MEPs)

There was widespread criticism from Labour MEPs, the Liberal Democrats and constitutional reform groups when the Labour government proposed to change the selecting and voting for UK MEPs to one which allowed parties rather than the electorate to select who was to be their MEP.

A position near the top of a party list would be crucial to success because seats would be allocated proportionately to the party, not the individual. 'Even moderate MEPs fear the list will be dominated by loyalists' {9}. But

> 'Labour took the unprecedented step of expelling two of its MEPs last night. ... Both have criticised welfare reform (cuts) and centrally-controlled candidates lists for next year's European elections.' {10}

> 'The Government (in its European Parliamentary Elections Bill) has insisted on a "closed list" system, allowing voters to choose only a party label, not an individual candidate - leaving the selection of would-be MEPs in the hands of the party bosses. This kind of centralisation breaks one of the cherished features of our democracy, namely the link between elector and elected. Under Labour's proposed system, our representatives will owe their place not to the voters, but to the apparatchiks who granted them a high place on the list.' {11}

Take-over Struggles

What is surprising is that these attempts to take over and control decision-taking processes appear more one-sided than would be the case if we were looking at unrelated chance events, at unrelated local

112

struggles. What is disturbing is that the pattern seems progressive as if it were planned.

So a continuing process appears to be taking place which seems to be aimed at concentrating decision-taking in the hands of the top-level party leadership.

Agreements Between Top-level Leaderships {4}

Also discussed in report 'Democracy Under Attack' {4} is how recently negotiated top-level trading agreements (GATT and the proposed MAI) appear to be taking away the control over key aspects of the internal affairs of participating countries. Taking control away from their elected governments, giving the control to multinational corporations.

But representatives, governments or government officials do not have the authority or right to reduce or sign away the participative (democratic) rights of the electors, of the population.

The 'General Agreement on Tariffs and Trade' (GATT)

GATT is a treaty between many countries in which they agreed that changed and new life-forms can be owned by multinational corporations, generation after generation. {6}

The GATT agreement apparently gives exclusive protection to patent holders for 20 years and imposes strict enforcement criteria. Huge royalty payments will have to be made to multinational corporations. 'Astonishingly, the rules place the onus of proof in case of dispute on the farmers, a provision going against normal rules of justice' {12}. The resulting costs could prevent the vast mass of small farmers from disputing the source of the seeds they are using. {6}

So multinational corporations have been given ownership over new life-forms and the power to force farmers world-wide to pay the multinational each year for seeds even when these seeds were grown by the farmer the previous year. {6}

It appears that GATT serves the interests of multinationals, that is of those who own and control them, at the expense of the economic and social interests and welfare of individual countries, of their people, of their citizens. {6}

And that a situation has been created in which the nature of profit-motivated and profit-orientated multinationals threatens human independence and freedom. {6}

'Ownership' has been defined as 'the right to possess an item of property' and so one has to look closely at where the right comes from and how it is exercised.

Ownership rights are the property of a country's citizens and communities {2}. As far as I know, as said before, no elected representative, government or government employee has the authority to hand over to multinational corporations (that is to those who own and control them), or to anyone else, such ownership rights.

So it would seem that the patent provisions of the GATT agreement are big-business-serving and arbitrary. {2, 6}

The 'Multilateral Agreement on Investment' (MAI)

MAI stands for 'Multilateral Agreement on Investment'. But its name does not reflect those aspects which are of deep concern. What is disturbing are not only the provisions of this proposed treaty but also that the provisions were debated in almost complete secrecy.

It appears that representatives of multinationals and governments representing the 29 richest industrialised countries, all OECD members, had been developing the MAI's provisions at the OECD (Organisation for Economic Co-operation and Development) since 1995. This seems to have been done in complete secrecy till a leaked copy became available on the Internet in 1997.

It seems that the agreement was to have been finalised in February 1998. Apparently it was adverse publicity relating to its restrictive provisions which delayed completion as concerned groups of citizens publicised their concerns. And some governments have now withdrawn their support.

So let us look at the kind of provisions this almost-agreed agreement on 'Multilateral Agreement on Investment' contained {7, 8}:

Democratically elected governments

> Would have had to allow multinationals access to the country.

> Would have been prevented from discriminating against foreign firms, would not be able to refuse any form of investment in any sector apart from defence.

> Would have been prevented from reducing or controlling a multinational's profits, say by minimum-wage or anti-pollution legislation, or by legislation to ensure local employment.

Multinationals would have the right to

> Sue national governments for any profits lost through laws which discriminated against the multinational, and which harmed a multinational's interests.

> Sue national governments in an international court which would have been closed to public scrutiny.

We saw that multinationals can legally avoid paying corporation tax by transfer pricing {5} and that unitary taxation {3, 5} can overcome this tax avoidance by assessing the actual profits being generated by a multinational in a particular country. Multinationals could, under MAI, have refused to be taxed by a system of unitary taxation.

Socially responsible and caring governmental legislation has to take precedence over the profit-motivated activities of corporations.

But it appears that under MAI the national governments would have handed over control, that is authority to act, over much of the economic and social welfare of their citizens to multinational corporations (that is to those who own and direct these corporations), if they had agreed to this treaty.

In other words, multinationals would have been given overriding authority over democratically elected governments.

Core Findings

It appears that GATT serves the interests of multinationals, that is of those who own and control them, at the expense of the economic and social interests and welfare of individual countries, of their people, of their citizens. {6}

So it would seem that the patent provisions of the GATT agreement are big-business-serving and arbitrary. {2, 6}

And that a situation has been created in which the nature of profit-motivated and profit-orientated multinationals threatens human independence and freedom. {6}

Socially responsible and caring governmental legislation has to take precedence over the profit-motivated activities of corporations.

But it appears that under MAI the national governments would have handed over control, that is authority to act, over much of the economic and social welfare of their citizens to multinational corporations (that is to those who own and direct these corporations), if they had agreed to this treaty.

In other words, multinationals would have been given overriding authority over democratically elected governments.

Conclusions

Social System

Top-level leadership, directors, are motivated by pay in its various forms, by greater wealth and by greater influence which includes dispensing patronage, and by power. The pay of directors is what owners decide to pay themselves and their directors, and increases with increasing influence and power. Considering mergers and take-overs, we see top-level leaderships battling with each other for more power, for greater control, over people and resources.

So the system is organised so that a few, a relatively very few, people at the top take the key decisions.

We see a pattern of differentials which rewards service to the owners and their establishment rather than ability or service to the community. The pay of directors is what owners decide to pay themselves.

Society and our activities are organised and controlled to enable possessions and wealth to be accumulated by a few people at the expense of the population.

What we see is a system where owners and top-level leaderships enrich themselves by taking or using and risking other people's moneys.

Corrupted Economics and Misleading Experts

Misleading biased interpretations and pronouncements are made in the name of 'economics' which relate to exploiting people at work, as citizens, and in the market place. It appears that misleading and inappropriate terms are used which confuse instead of illuminate, and which seem intended to confuse.

An expert is supposed to advise to the best of his ability, knowledge, skill and experience and is responsible, that is accountable, for the quality of his advice. Responsible, that is accountable, to those he is advising.

116

But employers have a strong influence on what their employees say in public and employees are likely to be advocating viewpoints which are employer-serving instead of being people-serving and community-serving.

Too often do experts tell people what the expert thinks is good for the people to do. Too often it is the expert who decides or who attempts to compel others to do as told.

Companies, Enterprises

Leaving aside economic theorising about what should be {15}, and looking only at what is actually taking place, we see that companies and enterprises are the means for exploiting not just the employees but the community and society as a whole for the benefit of only a few people at or near the top.

The source of profit (surplus) is money collected from customers, is money which belonged to customers.

Owners take the profits but have transferred much of their own risk to other people.

Without giving customers a choice, companies (owners) also simply take their customers' moneys

> for getting back money already spent on the business and

> for expanding the business without giving the community corresponding ownership rights.

Even co-operatives and mutual aid societies (building societies, credit unions) have been retaining some of their members' profits each year, for no apparent valid reason, accumulating these moneys for over 150 years <4>. By continually adding these moneys to their reserves they have become rich and powerful. Their chief executives and directors have become powerful, influential, and well paid.

Ownership laws which assign ownership 'rights' to owners have been devised by the owners themselves or by those who serve them.

No banker, no financial institution, no shareholder would dream of giving away their capital without making sure of retaining ownership and control over this money, through the transfer of corresponding securities and ownership rights, and of direct and indirect participation in the resulting profits.

But all the above mentioned moneys are being taken legally from customers who are the owners of these moneys by the owners of corporations. They are taken by corporations (their owners) without in return giving corresponding ownership rights to their customers or the community.

Ownership of land and means of production, of funds and wealth, has always been accumulated at someone else's expense. All belonged to the community, belonged to all alike.

Company pension funds in the UK run into many GBP billions and between them own, and thus are in position to influence and control, much if not most of UK's equities. Including company credit unions and providers of private pensions, such moneys and funds represent the working population's savings.

Instead of being under the control of those who contributed, these moneys are in effect placed under the control of a few people at the top who in this way gain power and influence, are enabled to dispense patronage (and support each other), gain high incomes and much wealth.

Role of Government

Government serves business enterprises (companies, owners) by

>   Transferring taxpayers' moneys to enterprises.

>   Condoning tax avoidance by enterprises (making good the loss by collecting more taxes from the population).

>   Using taxpayers' moneys to pay operating costs of enterprises.

It serves business enterprises and the rich by

>   Condoning tax avoidance by the rich.

>   Taxing the working population more severely.

So we see taxpayers' moneys being used in different ways to enlarge the profits of companies and thus of their owners, and to make the rich even richer.

Vast amounts are handed over yearly in such ways and increase the wealth and power of a small number of people without any corresponding return to the community. They are generally given without a corresponding transfer of ownership rights and control to those who provided the money, to the community.

Profit (Exploitation) Maximising

In practice directors are generally required by owner-serving laws to act first and foremost in the interests of the owners, so that it is profit which is maximised. Short-term and long-term profits can be and are being maximised.

Profits are then maximised regardless of the cost and consequences to the community, limited only by the likelihood of unpleasant consequences such as restraining fines, punitive legal punishment or adverse publicity.

Profit margins and prices need to be controlled effectively so as to protect the community from exploitation. But they are not.

Owners and employers use inflation as an excuse for reducing real wages and salaries of the working population so as to increase profits.

And employees do not receive their share of the increasing national income and wealth. UK pensions, for example, would now have to be increased by 34 percent just to reach the level at which they should be.

Apparently owners and employers will, when they can, pressurise the working population into accepting even lower rates of pay by increasing the working population's needs. Doing so by advocating greater unemployment, reducing social security, reducing national health service provisions, weakening the quality of education (knowledge, clear thinking, understanding, objective evaluation).

Moneys saved by government by spending less on social security for those in need and moneys gained by collecting more tax from the working population, are apparently being used by owner-serving governments to reduce the taxes collected from the rich and from companies.

In addition, purchasing power is being transferred from the bottom to the top. It has been estimated that 10 percent of the UK population were sinking into direct poverty, any gains in income being overtaken by the increasing cost of living. The next 20 percent were losing out, were being reduced to relative poverty.

On the other hand the top 0.4 percent of the population took gains in take-home purchasing power which were 100 times those received by the general population. The large top-level remuneration has been increasing yearly for some years at up to four or five times the rate of inflation, increasing each year by amounts many times exceeding the average income of the working population.

So profits are apparently being maximised regardless of the cost to others, to the community. Without care or concern for the condition, standard of living or quality of life of the working population. Without being concerned about the enormous human suffering which results.

Overall, what we see are consequences of decisions made at the top, and the results of putting them into effect. Results and consequences which at times make the decisions seem so brutal that they appear inhuman.

Authoritarian Struggle to Take Over and Control Decision-making by Transferring it to Leaders

Authoritarian minds attempt to take over and place democratically controlled organisations under authoritarian control. They do so by struggling to take over the decision-taking in the management and control of companies, enterprises and all types of community organisations.

The confrontation between on the one hand elected policy-making bodies, and on the other hand those who are supposed to put their policies into effect, can be seen in many areas.

We can see the struggle in all organisations and at all levels. It is a struggle against authoritarian management or government for the right to take decisions. And in all democratic organisations it is a struggle against the authoritarian mind taking over the decision-taking.

A continuous battle is taking place between on the one hand policy-deciding by the many through elected assemblies, and on the other hand policy-deciding at the top, by a few. This is clearly shown by the way in which full-time officials and executives attempt to take power away from their policy-setting assemblies, after which they attempt to impose their will on the membership or population.

The government's important role of keeping the system in operation and of transferring such vast funds from the working population to leaderships, explains the intense struggle going on within political parties for control of decision-taking (policy-setting), with authoritarian minds attempting to concentrate decision-taking in the hands of the top-level party leadership.

These attempts to take over and control decision-taking processes are far more one-sided than would be the case if we were looking at unrelated chance events, at unrelated local struggles. At times the pattern seems progressive as if it were planned.

Agreements Between Top-level Leaderships

Recently negotiated top-level trading agreements (GATT and the proposed MAI) appear to be taking away the control over key aspects of the internal affairs of participating countries. Taking control away from their elected governments, giving the control to multinational corporations.

But representatives, governments or government officials do not have the authority or right to reduce or sign away the participative (democratic) rights of the electors, of the population.

No elected representative, government or government employee has the authority

1. to hand over to corporations (that is to those who own and control them), or to anyone else, an overriding control over the present and future, economic and social, welfare of the people, or

2. to sign away democratic rights of their people for the self-determination of key fundamental aspects of their lives.

It appears that the 'General Agreement on Tariffs and Trade' (GATT) serves the interests of multinationals, that is of those who own and control them, at the expense of the economic and social interests and welfare of individual countries, of their people, of their citizens.

And it would seem that the patent provisions of the GATT agreement are big-business-serving and arbitrary.

MAI stands for 'Multilateral Agreement on Investment'. But its name does not reflect those aspects which are of deep concern.

What is disturbing are not only the provisions of this proposed treaty but also that the provisions were debated in complete secrecy till a leaked copy became available on the Internet in 1997. Apparently it was adverse publicity relating to its restrictive provisions which delayed completion as concerned groups of citizens publicised their concerns. And some governments have now withdrawn their support.

It appears that under MAI the national governments would have handed over control, that is authority to act, over much of the economic and social welfare of their citizens to multinational corporations (that is to those who own and direct these corporations), if they had agreed to this treaty.

In other words, multinationals would have been given overriding authority over democratically elected governments.

Socially responsible and caring governmental legislation has to take precedence over the profit-motivated activities of corporations.

Secrecy and Publicity

We saw that the MAI's provisions were discussed in complete secrecy and that it was adverse publicity relating to its restrictive provisions which delayed completion of the MAI as concerned groups of citizens publicised their concerns. We also saw that consequently some governments withdrew support.

A company can serve as a front behind which those who take key decisions can hide, as a front for owners and directors.

And the most effective control of corporate irresponsibility appears to be the fear of bad publicity, of public awareness of socially irresponsible company behaviour, of consequent impact on sales and market share.

Particularly so when publicity names those responsible for making antisocial decisions within the company, and those responsible for condoning, or for omitting to restrain, the company's antisocial activities.

Overall

So profits are apparently being maximised regardless of the cost to others, to the community. Without care or concern for the condition, standard of living or quality of life of the working population. Without being concerned about the enormous human suffering which results.

What we see are consequences of decisions made at the top, and the results of putting them into effect. Results and consequences which at times make the decisions seem so brutal that they appear inhuman.

Attempts to take over and control decision-taking processes are far more one-sided and widespread than would be the case if we were looking at unrelated chance events, at unrelated local struggles. At times the pattern seems progressive as if it were planned.

We can see struggle in all organisations and at all levels. It is a struggle against authoritarian management or government for the right to take decisions. And in all democratic organisations it is a struggle against the authoritarian mind taking over the decision-taking.

Notes and References

Notes

<1> Note that what is said in this report mostly applies equally well to companies, corporations, businesses or enterprises. Within the context of this report these terms are usually interchangeable although companies (corporations) are registered (incorporated), their owners then benefiting from limited liability.

<2> Extracted from {4} which discusses the meaning of democracy, and its necessary requirements, in more detail.

<3> See also {16} for a more comprehensive discussion of the electing, appointing and appraisal of managers, directors and elected representatives, the right to know, the right to be heard, and of work, pay and differentials.

<4> Since I discovered this and published my findings {16} there have been isolated instances of co-operatives moving towards giving their members a better deal.

<5> Costs + Profit = Price

'Mark-up' is 'Profit' expressed as a percentage of 'Costs'

Say   Costs = 100
           Profit = 10

Then   Price = 100+10=110

And   Mark-up = (10/100)*100 = 10 percent

'Costs' include wages and salaries

References

{ 1}   See chapter 14:
       'Corrupted Economics and Misguided (Misleading) Experts'
       Manfred Davidmann

{ 2}   See chapter 12:
        'Understanding How Society is Organised for
        Controlling and Exploiting People'
        Manfred Davidmann

{ 3}   See chapter 13:
        'Taxing the Population for Private Profit'
        Manfred Davidmann

{ 4}   See chapter 11:
        'Democracy Under Attack: Top-level Leadership
        and Decision-making'
        Manfred Davidmann

{ 5}   See chapter 8:
        'Transfer Pricing and Taxation'
        Manfred Davidmann

{ 6}   See chapter 9:
        'Creating, Patenting and Marketing of New Forms
        of Life'
        Manfred Davidmann

{ 7}   Globalisers run into the buffers
        Larry Elliott and Charlotte Denny
        Guardian, 24/03/98

{ 8}   Move to revive world pact
        Larry Elliott
        Guardian, 10/09/98

{ 9}   Labour MEPs face cull; Row looms over Blairite
        poll lists
        Michael White
        Guardian, 27/12/97

{10}   Labour expels rebel MEPs
        Stephen Bates
        Guardian, 09/01/98

{11}   Editorial
        Guardian, 20/11/98

{12}   Seeds of discontent
        Walter Schwarz
        Guardian, 11/03/94

{13}   In 'Management and Leadership:
       Local, National, Multinational (Global),
       Principles and Practice'
       Manfred Davidmann
       ISBN 978-0-85192-057-3
       See chapter 4: 'Motivation'

{14}   See chapter 16:
       'The Will to Work: What People Struggle to
       Achieve'
       Manfred Davidmann

{15}   Community Economics: Principles
       Manfred Davidmann, 1992, 1996
       solhaam.org

{16}   'Cooperatives and Cooperation:
       Causes of Failure, Guidelines for Success'
       Manfred Davidmann
       ISBN 978-0-85192-056-6

Chapter 11

Democracy Under Attack: Top-level Leadership and Decision-making

Summary

Discusses and illustrates the internal struggles taking place in companies (corporations), political parties and other organisations, for achieving greater democracy and against those wishing to overpower democratic processes of decision-taking.

Describes participative organisation (democracy), the basic criteria by which it can be judged and the processes by which leaderships attempt to take over the decision-taking processes.

Also discusses how recently negotiated top-level trading agreements (GATT and the proposed MAI) appear to be taking control over key aspects of the internal affairs of participating countries away from their elected governments, giving the control to multinational corporations.

Introduction

This is one of a series of four studies which were undertaken to obtain a better understanding of why people have to struggle throughout their adult lives, in all countries and organisations, at all levels, to maintain and improve their standard of living and quality of life.

We know what people are struggling to achieve {3, 34} and so these studies explore why people have to struggle by looking at what they are struggling against.

The main report 'What People are Struggling Against' (See chapter 10) brings together the work reported in the four component studies by extracting and rearranging key findings from them.

To get an overview, it would be best to read the main report first. If you want more information on particular aspects of interest, you could then go to the component studies (See chapter 11, 12, 13 and 14).

Participative Organisation: The Meaning of 'Democracy'

Words like 'democracy' and 'democratic' can be used to imply that a system of government or management is socially fair and caring, and 'of, by and for the people', when this is not the case.

Hence the need to look at the meaning of 'democracy'.

Participative (democratic) organisation rests on the population electing representatives, on the basis of each person having one vote, for putting into effect policies decided by the population. Representatives are responsible to, and accountable to, the population for what they do or omit to do, and for the way in which they do this.

What underlies participative organisation (democracy) is decision-taking by the people at the level of the people.

A representative is selected by those whom he will represent so that his authority stems from those who elected him. The source of his authority is the consent of the managed to be managed or of the ruled to be ruled.

They hold him accountable by withdrawing their consent, by in the end electing someone else.

In the management area by the withdrawal of labour. In the area of government, by withdrawing co-operation from the political party or government by protesting, demonstrating, withdrawing support, replacing the party hierarchy or the government. {4}

And representatives, governments or government officials do not have the authority or right to change or sign away the participative (democratic) rights of the electors, of the population.

Policies state what has to be done and by when it has to be done. What needs to be stressed is that in a participative (democratic) organisation policies are decided by a well-informed population at the level of the population and that policies then become binding on management or government. <2>

In an authoritarian organisation the policy decisions are taken at the top or near the top by the hierarchy (establishment) and are binding on the organisation's members. Decision-taking at the top is sometimes referred to as 'deciding centrally'. Authoritarian organisation is the opposite of democracy and underlies dictatorship. {4}

And what we see is conflict between authoritarian minds wishing to dominate, control and exploit on the one hand and, on the other hand, citizens wishing to maintain and improve the standard of living and quality of life for the population as a whole by democratic (grassroots level) decision-taking.

So the real struggle is not between political left and right, but is a struggle for participation (the right to take decisions).

We can see the struggle in all organisations and at all levels. It is a struggle against authoritarian management or government for the right to take decisions. And in all democratic organisations it is a struggle against the authoritarian mind taking over the decision-taking. {3}

A continuous battle is taking place between on the one hand policy-deciding by the many through elected assemblies, and on the other hand policy-deciding at the top, by a few. This is clearly shown by the way in which full-time officials and executives attempt to take power away from their policy-setting assemblies, after which they attempt to impose their will on the membership or population.

The confrontation between on the one hand elected policy-making bodies, and on the other hand those who are supposed to put their policies into effect, can be seen in many areas.

We are here looking at decision-taking in the management and control of companies, corporations, enterprises and all types of community organisations. Looking at the ways in which authoritarian minds attempt to take over and place democratically controlled organisations under authoritarian control.

This is an age-old problem we need to be aware of so as to counter it effectively, and the following sections look at how this struggle manifests itself.

Top-level Leadership Taking Over Decision-making in Business, Service and Community Organisations

Majority Shareholder Taking Over Decision-making from Other Shareholders

A majority shareholder can decide who, apart from himself, is appointed to the board of directors. In this way he determines the policy of the enterprise and thus top-level decisions. To that extent he takes possession of the ownership rights of the other shareholders and can use the company's assets for his own ends. Other shareholders may then have little say or interest in deciding policy or in the running of the company. What is left for them to decide is whether to sell the shares they hold or whether to buy more. {5, 14}

Trade Union General Secretary or Leader of Political Party Changing the Rules to Increase Personal Power

Another example is that of the trade union General Secretary or of the leader of a political party who after being elected attempts to change the rules so as to make his appointment more secure or permanent. {3}

Doing so to stay in power regardless of how ineffectively he may be serving the members who elected him, doing so to avoid offering himself for re-election at regular short intervals. Attempting to take away from the membership, who in effect employ him, the right of any employer to appraise and evaluate performance. Preventing them from expressing support or disapproval by the extent to which they support or wish to replace him.

Reorganising the National Health Service: Replacing Grassroots Decision-making with Top-level Direction and Control of Spending

Health service policies were decided by a process of consultation and participation at all levels. This process worked well and provided the kind of effective treatments and services needed by patients and the community, whose needs were expressed by and through various Community Health Councils, Joint Staff Consultative Committees and community organisations. {1}

A conservative government began to reorganise the British National Health Service (NHS) in 1984. The planned changes appeared to run counter to good management practice and were likely to greatly reduce the effectiveness of the NHS {1}.

However, the government went ahead and the changes were made. The making of policy decisions at local levels by local management teams was replaced by what appeared to be a rigid system of direction from, and accountability to, the top. It became apparent that direction and budgetary control from the top was taking precedence over and replacing local policy setting by teamwork, that higher authority was to decide what and how much was to be done for patients and community.

Controlling the Use of Capital: User-owned User-benefiting Bank Converted to Profit-motivated Shareholder-benefiting Ownership

The Trustee Savings Bank (TSB) was run for the benefit of its depositors. Massive funds were serving the working population and the community, were a source of strength and support. Trustees held the Bank 'upon Trust' for the depositors who in turn could appoint and remove trustees. The use of these funds was in effect being controlled by depositors, by the working population.

A conservative government decided to convert the TSB into a shareholder-owned profit-maximising bank just like the commercial banks, by selling ('privatising') it.

> 'As there was deemed to be no owner to receive the purchase money, buyers received not only ownership of the bank but also the money they bought it with.' <3> {13}

The funds were thus placed under the control of people who would be more likely to maximise profits for the new owners than to consider the money-needs of the working population.

Senior Executives Taking Over from Owners: Co-operatives

Co-operatives belong to their members and operate for the benefit of their members. Policies are decided by members at general meetings held at regular intervals. Agreed policies are mandatory, have to be put into effect. Directors are elected from the membership and their role is to have these policies put into effect by the Chief Executive and managers. {2}

In the Mondragon co-operatives the policy setting and control of management activities have apparently moved away from owners (producers, workers) towards an upper level of senior executives. {11}

More information on the internal confrontations within co-operatives and mutual societies can be found in {2} and in associated case-studies on Building Societies {8}, Kibbutzim {12} and the John Lewis Partnership {15}.

Senior Executives Taking Over from Owners: Companies (Corporations)

Owners (Shareholders) balance the power of the Chief Executive and of executive directors by appointing part-time directors which correspond to community-representatives on decision-taking bodies.

Consider the Chief Executive or Managing Director of a company who, with the other executive company directors, controls the company's day-to-day activities and whose job it is to put into effect the policy of the Board of Directors.

Executive directors, generally being heads of departments, are responsible for their day-to-day work to the Managing Director. They are thus unlikely to contradict him in the Boardroom, and are unlikely to criticise their own results and their own efficiency.

So shareholders balance the decision-taking power of the executive (full-time) directors by appointing outside (part-time) directors to the Board. Part-time directors, when completely independent of the chief executive (managing director), can be relied on to represent shareholders' interests, to criticise on behalf of the shareholders what the executives are doing. {3 <1>}

Employee Participation in Decision-making

The policy-making body of the Histadrut, Israel's general federation of trade unions, decided some time ago that worker participation in decision taking was to be introduced in the Histadrut's own enterprises. Twenty years later the workers in Histadrut-owned enterprises still had a long way to go before achieving this. {3}

Top-level Leadership Taking Over Decision-making from the Population: Britain's Labour Party 1997/98

What follows is based on newspaper reports <4> and articles which seemed relevant to this discussion of the ongoing struggle to maintain and improve democratic rights within the democracies.

We are looking at recent and ongoing events and it is difficult to separate facts from opinions. However, an overall pattern emerges which appears to reinforce and strengthen what is said here about top-level leadership attempting to take over decision-taking from the grassroots population, about the consequent struggle in all organisations and at all levels.

What is surprising is that these attempts to take over and control decision-taking processes appear more one-sided than would be the case if we were looking at unrelated chance events, at unrelated local struggles. What is disturbing is that the pattern seems progressive as if it were planned.

Deciding What is to be Done

Taking Over from the People: Labour Party's Annual Conference

In 1979 the UKs oil wells started to produce and the UK became a net exporter of oil, as far as I know the only one of the industrialised countries to be producing more oil than it consumed, extremely well off as a result. A conservative (Tory) government was elected in the same year, harvesting the benefits and staying in power for 18 years. But by 1997 poverty and wealth differentials had increased by so much, and the rights and social security of the working population had been reduced to such an extent, that it was clear that this time the Labour party would be elected.

Before the general election (May 1997) the Labour party's leadership changed and under the new leadership some fundamental changes were introduced.

The Annual Conference of the Labour party consisted of delegates from local branches and was policy setting. Resolutions, proposed policies, were submitted by local Labour party branches, debated by delegates at the conference. If passed then it was up to the party's executive (its leadership) to implement the policy, to put it into effect. The decisions were mandatory, had to be put into effect.

So the Labour party's annual conference took binding decisions on policy proposals brought up by grassroots membership. They decided policy which the executive had to follow and put into effect.

In the autumn of 1997 the conference voted for a system which transferred the choice of what could be debated from grassroots membership to a policy commission chaired by the party leader {16}. This in effect took away a vital aspect of decision-taking from the working population and placed it in the hands of leader and leadership.

In January 1998 it was announced that forty-five policy forums were to be set up in which members would be invited to express their views on policies, from social issues to local government and that such views should eventually work through to the annual party conference.

Although members would be able to discuss policy, it seems the leadership can either take note or else ignore the proceedings. {17}

The annual conference ceased to decide policies, ceased to decide what had to be done. Instead of deciding mandatory policies based on direct policy proposals from local branches, the annual conference became a talking-shop, discussing and expressing views on subjects selected and approved by the leadership.

So a continuing process appears to be taking place which seems to be aimed at concentrating decision-taking in the hands of the top-level party leadership.

Serving Big Business: New Labour

The leader of the Labour party is apparently determined
> to forge an alliance between Labour and the business community, banishing the old image of Labour as the party of the unions. {18}

In a hard-hitting and relevant article, Paul Foot points to the differences between social-democratic pro-people policies and those of a market system in which irresponsible corporations have economic power. {19}

He makes the point that when British social democratic leaders became Prime Ministers
> 'they set off enthusiastically in pursuit of the mildest possible reforms of the market system. Then .. they found themselves .. blown off course .. . So they turned round and set off in the opposite direction.' 'Once this subservience to the market becomes clear, so do all the other rather apparently inexplicable actions of the government.'

In September 1998 an opinion poll reported that the majority of people felt that the leader of the Labour government was closer to big business than to ordinary people. {20}

Telling Elected Representatives How to Vote and How to Behave: Members of Parliament (MPs)

> 'Labour MPs who persistently defy the party line at Westminster can expect the chief whip <5> to send a report to their constituencies which could determine whether or not they are deselected, according to plans adopted yesterday.' {21}

Which is softened a little by
>'A constituency which receives a bad report from Labour's chief
>whip ... will take its own decision to deselect or endorse its
>local member.' {21}

So in effect the local parties are to be informed of the extent to which their MP follows policies determined by the party leadership.

Censoring and Silencing Alternative ('Opposing') Points of View: The Labour Party's National Executive Council (NEC)

The Labour government's proposals for changing the UKs system for electing its MEPs (Members of European Parliament) led to the temporary suspension of four Labour MEPs, apparently because they discussed in public the merits of different systems of proportional representation, favouring as more democratic a system disliked by their party. {22}

The Labour party then 'took the unprecedented step' of expelling two of its MEPs because they argued against the party's proposals for centrally-controlled candidates lists for next year's European elections. {24}
>'Even moderate MEPs fear the list will be dominated by
>loyalists'. {23}

It was also unprecedented when in May 1998 the Labour party's MPs were told by their party whips <5> to tell their local parties who to nominate for the next elections to the Party's National Executive Council. {25}

MPs had been told that the ballot for places on the NEC would be in secret but
>MPs and Euro-MPs protested when they discovered their ballot
>papers were numbered and complained that Millbank (the
>Labour Party's head office) would be able to trace who had
>voted for leftwing candidates. {26}

It seems that the Labour Party leadership had been campaigning against 'leftwing' candidates. However, four 'Grassroots Alliance' members were elected to Labour's NEC.

One of these newly elected members, Liz Davies, said
>On the NEC, we will do our best to ensure that debate in the
>party is conducted in an open, tolerant and inclusive manner
>and that party members are genuinely consulted and involved
>in decision-making. {20}

So the new NEC contains at least four members likely to be speaking for matters of concerns to grassroots members and who may be publicising their points of view so as to inform and consult party members.

Before the first meeting of the new NEC, a party official asked NEC members to agree to an unprecedented rule ('guidance') {27, 28}

> which would require them to inform the party's press office "before discussing NEC business with the media".

Also

> "NEC members should try to avoid going head on head with another NEC member and, where possible, with another member of the Labour Party."

And

> ... a veteran former NEC figure protested: "Party officials would never have dared tell senior MPs and trade unionists what to do. The NEC would have discussed something like this and instructed officials. Now they seem to be instructing us."

It seems to me that breaches of these guidance rules would be noticed and tell against the individual with party leadership. And it looks as if NEC members should not argue with each other or with other party members in public.

I do not see how Labour party members could find out about alternative proposals or viewpoints except by them being discussed openly in the media.

There appear to have been

> widespread protests against (the) draft code restricting NEC access to the media {29}

and Liz Davies' comments on the draft code were reported as

> "It seems to be designed to stop the constituency members of the NEC, elected by ordinary Labour party members, from speaking (their) mind," Ms Davies said. "If we shut up, party members will find out what happened at the NEC from the Millbank (Labour Party head office) machine ... . I don't think that's acceptable." {29}

136

Selecting and Electing Representatives: UK Members of European Parliament (MEPs)

Proportional Representation: 'Closed-list' and 'Open-list' Systems

Voting by proportional representation (PR) decides how many candidates of a party are elected. If 300 seats are available and the party gets one-third of the votes, then it gets one-third of the seats, that is it gets 100 seats.

If the party put forward a list of 300 candidates, only 100 can become representatives.

With a "closed list" system of PR, the electors vote for the party and not for a local candidate. They thus vote for the party's list. In the above example, it is the first-named 100 names on the list which become representatives.

With an "open list" system the electors have the chance of voting for candidates of their choice from the party's list.

Closed-list System

Whether or not one is placed on the list, and one's position on the list, determines whether one is elected or not.

With this system it is not really the electorate which decides whether one is elected as a local representative. Whether one is elected depends on whether one is placed on the list and on one's top-to-bottom position on the list. So whether one is elected depends on the party leader or leadership.

So one's chance of being elected depends on doing as told by leader or leadership, on supporting their policies, instead of depending on serving one's constituents (local electors), instead of being responsible and accountable to the electors, to the community one is supposed to represent and act for.

The higher up one's name appears on the list, the more likely is one to be elected, the more likely is it that one benefits from the high salary, excellent allowances, good working conditions and good pension rights which go with the job. Loyalty to leader or leadership replaces loyalty to electors.

It is the grassroots membership which should select and decide who is to represent them. The party leadership seems to be close to taking over both functions.

What we see taking place with a closed-list system is far removed from being responsible and accountable to one's local electors, to the local community, for the way in which one represents them and looks after their interests both at local and national level. Democratic decision-taking is reversed by a system of closed-list proportional representation as decision-taking by representatives is replaced with obedience to dictates from the top.

UK Members of European Parliament (MEPs)

There was widespread criticism from Labour MEPs, the Liberal Democrats and constitutional reform groups when the Labour government proposed to change the selecting and voting for UK MEPs to one which allowed parties rather than the electorate to select who was to be their MEP. And

> 'The proposals led to the temporary suspension of four Labour MEPs who violated a ban, under a new party code of conduct, on publicly debating the type of proportional representation they wanted Labour to adopt.' {22}

A position near the top of a party list would be crucial to success because seats would be allocated proportionately to the party, not the individual. 'Even moderate MEPs fear the list will be dominated by loyalists' {23}. But

> 'Labour took the unprecedented step of expelling two of its MEPs last night. ... Both have criticised welfare reform (cuts) and centrally-controlled candidates' lists for next year's European elections.' {24}

> 'The Government (in its European Parliamentary Elections Bill) has insisted on a "closed list" system, allowing voters to choose only a party label, not an individual candidate - leaving the selection of would-be MEPs in the hands of the party bosses. This kind of centralisation breaks one of the cherished features of our democracy, namely the link between elector and elected. Under Labour's proposed system, our representatives will owe their place not to the voters, but to the apparatchiks who granted them a high place on the list.' {30}

In Israel the democratic system of proportional representation has been defeated by the way in which prospective members of the Knesset (government) are selected by party hierarchies and also by the way in which, after an election, minority parties can combine to replace the majority party. {3}

Reason would suggest that the largest parties should get together and compromise.

Agreements Between Top-level Leaderships

The 'General Agreement on Tariffs and Trade' (GATT)

GATT is a treaty between many countries in which they agreed that changed and new life-forms can be owned by multinational corporations, generation after generation. {7}

The GATT agreement apparently gives exclusive protection to patent holders for 20 years and imposes strict enforcement criteria. Huge royalty payments will have to be made to multinational corporations. 'Astonishingly, the rules place the onus of proof in case of dispute on the farmers, a provision going against normal rules of justice' {31}. The resulting costs could prevent the vast mass of small farmers from disputing the source of the seeds they are using. {7}

So multinational corporations have been given ownership over new life-forms and the power to force farmers world-wide to pay the multinational each year for seeds even when these seeds were grown by the farmer the previous year. {7}

It appears that GATT serves the interests of multinationals, that is of those who own and control them, at the expense of the economic and social interests and welfare of individual countries, of their people, of their citizens. {7}

And that a situation has been created in which the nature of profit-motivated and profit-orientated multinationals threatens human independence and freedom. {7}

In 1998 a US multinational 'announced plans to unravel the entire human genetic code by 2001', saying it intended to patent 'the most valuable gene sequences', and to sell the information to scientific institutions and drug companies. {32}

Combining this information with recent developments concerning the cloning of animals and human beings raises disturbing and even fearful prospects.

'Ownership' has been defined as 'the right to possess an item of property' and so one has to look closely at where the right comes from and how it is exercised.

Ownership rights are the property of a country's citizens and communities {14}. As far as I know, no elected representative, government or government employee has the authority to hand over to multinational corporations (that is to those who own and control them), or to anyone else, such ownership rights.

So it would seem that the patent provisions of the GATT agreement are big-business-serving and arbitrary. {14, 7}

The 'Multilateral Agreement on Investment' (MAI)

MAI stands for 'Multilateral Agreement on Investment'. But its name does not reflect those aspects which are of deep concern. What is disturbing are not only the provisions of this proposed treaty but also that the provisions were debated in almost complete secrecy.

It appears that representatives of multinationals and governments representing the 29 richest industrialised countries, all OECD members, had been developing the MAI's provisions at the OECD (Organisation for Economic Co-operation and Development) since 1995. This seems to have been done in complete secrecy till a leaked copy became available on the Internet in 1997.

It seems that the agreement was to have been finalised in February 1998. Apparently it was adverse publicity relating to its restrictive provisions which delayed completion as concerned groups of citizens publicised their concerns. And some governments have now withdrawn their support.

So let us look at the kind of provisions this almost-agreed agreement on 'Multilateral Agreement on Investment' contained {9, 10}:

Democratically elected governments

- Would have had to allow multinationals access to the country.

- Would have been prevented from discriminating against foreign firms, would not be able to refuse any form of investment in any sector apart from defence.

- Would have been prevented from reducing or controlling a multinationals profits, say by minimum-wage or anti-pollution legislation, or by legislation to ensure local employment.

Multinationals would have had the right to

- Sue national governments for any profits lost through laws which discriminated against the multinational, and which harmed a multinational's interests.

- Sue national governments in an international court which would have been closed to public scrutiny.

We saw that multinationals can legally avoid paying corporation tax by transfer pricing {6} and that unitary taxation <6> {6, 33} can overcome this tax avoidance by assessing the actual profits being generated by a multinational in a particular country. Multinationals could, under MAI, have refused to be taxed by a system of unitary taxation.

Socially responsible and caring governmental legislation has to take precedence over the profit-motivated activities of corporations.

But it appears that under MAI the national governments would have handed over control, that is authority to act, over much of the economic and social welfare of their citizens to multinational corporations (that is to those who own and direct these corporations), if they had agreed to this treaty.

In other words, multinationals would have been given overriding authority over democratically elected governments.

As far as I know, no elected representative, government or government employee has the authority

1. to hand over to corporations (that is to those who own and control them), or to anyone else, an overriding control over the present and future, economic and social, welfare of its people, or

2. to sign away the democratic rights of their people for the self-determination of key fundamental aspects of their lives.

Notes and References

Notes

<1> See {3}: Appendix 1: The Struggle for Independence in the Boardrooms, Government, Trade Unions and other Institutions.

<2> For a comprehensive discussion of the electing, appointing and appraisal of managers, directors and elected representatives, of the right to ownership, the right to know, the right to be heard, and of work, pay and differentials, see also {2}.

<3>   See also {14}

<4>   Drawn from one newspaper which, however, has a
      reputation for informed, investigative and fair
      reporting.

<5>   The Labour party's Chief Whip and his deputy are
      apparently elected by the party's MPs. Whips are
      paid when their party is in office and tell their
      party's MPs what the party leadership wants them to
      do. Their loyalty would be to the party leadership.

<6>   See {33}: 'Condoning Tax Avoidance by the Rich.'

References

{ 1}   Reorganising the National Health Service:
       An Evaluation of the Griffiths Report
       Manfred Davidmann, 1984, 1995
       solhaam.org

{ 2}   'Cooperatives and Cooperation:
       Causes of Failure, Guidelines for Success'
       Manfred Davidmann
       ISBN 978-0-85192-056-6

{ 3}   See chapter 16:
       'The Will to Work: What People Struggle to
       Achieve'
       Manfred Davidmann

{ 4}   In 'Management and Leadership:
       Local, National, Multinational (Global),
       Principles and Practice'
       Manfred Davidmann
       ISBN 978-0-85192-057-3
       See chapter 2: 'Style of Management and
       Leadership'

{ 5}   See chapter 5,
       'Ownership and Deciding Policy: Companies,
       Shareholders, Directors and Community'
       Manfred Davidmann

{ 6}   See chapter 8:
        'Transfer Pricing and Taxation'
        Manfred Davidmann

{ 7}   See chapter 9:
        'Creating, Patenting and Marketing of New Forms
        of Life'
        Manfred Davidmann

{ 8}   In 'Cooperatives and Cooperation:
        Causes of Failure, Guidelines for Success'
        Manfred Davidmann
        ISBN 978-0-85192-056-6
        See chapter 5.3: 'Building Societies'

{ 9}   Globalisers run into the buffers
        Larry Elliott and Charlotte Denny
        Guardian, 24/03/98

{10}   Move to revive world pact
        Larry Elliott
        Guardian, 10/09/98

{11}   In 'Cooperatives and Cooperation:
        Causes of Failure, Guidelines for Success'
        Manfred Davidmann
        ISBN 978-0-85192-056-6
        See chapter 5.7: 'Mondragon Co-operatives
        (Mondragon Corporacion Cooperativa)'

{12}   In 'Cooperatives and Cooperation:
        Causes of Failure, Guidelines for Success'
        Manfred Davidmann
        ISBN 978-0-85192-056-6
        See chapter 5.8: 'Kibbutzim'

{13}   In 'Cooperatives and Cooperation:
        Causes of Failure, Guidelines for Success'
        Manfred Davidmann
        ISBN 978-0-85192-056-6
        See chapter 5.1: 'The Trustee Savings Bank
        Give-Away'

{14}   See chapter 12:
       'Understanding How Society is Organised for
       Controlling and Exploiting People'
       Manfred Davidmann

{15}   In 'Cooperatives and Cooperation:
       Causes of Failure, Guidelines for Success'
       Manfred Davidmann
       ISBN 978-0-85192-056-6
       See chapter 5.6: 'John Lewis Partnership PLC'

{16}   The heirs to Trotsky
       Mark Seddon (Editor of Tribune)
       Guardian, 11/08/97

{17}   Labour gives grassroots a voice: Forums hand
       policy-making power to ordinary members
       Ewen MacAskill
       Guardian, 02/01/98

{18}   Blair opens Lords attack
       Ewen MacAskill
       Guardian, 02/08/97

{19}   Nasty dose of contagion
       Paul Foot
       Guardian, 22/09/98

{20}   So there is an alternative
       Liz Davies
       Guardian, 28/09/98

{21}   Labour whip plans new crackdown on dissident
       MPs
       Michael White and Anne Perkins
       Guardian, 19/05/98

{22}   Straw retreats over option for PR pol
       David Hencke
       Guardian, 26/11/97

{23}   Labour MEPs face cull; Row looms over Blairite
       poll lists
       Michael White
       Guardian, 27/12/97

{24}   Labour expels rebel MEPs
       Stephen Bates
       Guardian, 09/01/98

{25}   Labour whip plans new crackdown on dissident
       MPs
       Michael White and Anne Perkins
       Guardian, 19/05/98

{26}   MPs cry foul on ballot
       Ewen MacAskill
       Guardian, 30/09/98

{27}   Labour gag on NEC members
       Michael White
       Guardian, 13/11/98

{28}   Davies the lone rebel on NEC rules: Scaled-down
       control 'guidance' wins backing
       Michael White
       Guardian, 18/11/98

{29}   Peers defied as vote bill returns to Lords again
       Michael White
       Guardian, 14/11/98

{30}   Editorial
       Guardian, 20/11/98

{31}   Seeds of discontent
       Walter Schwarz
       Guardian, 11/03/94

{32}   US company plans to patent key gene codes
       Paul Brown and Martin Walker
       Guardian, 13/05/98

{33}   See chapter 13:
       'Taxing the Population for Private Profit'
       Manfred Davidmann

{34}   In 'Management and Leadership:
       Local, National, Multinational (Global),
       Principles and Practice'
       Manfred Davidmann
       ISBN 978-0-85192-057-3
       See chapter 4: 'Motivation'

Chapter 12

Understanding How Society is Organised for Controlling and Exploiting People

Summary

Describes the various ways in which corporations (companies) accumulate their capital and reserves from moneys taken from customers. Enterprises are allowed to collect, take over and control such moneys and co-operatives also take over moneys from their members.

The report looks at ownership, at the right to own property, and at the way society and our activities are organised and controlled to enable possessions and wealth to be accumulated by a few people at the expense of the population.

Introduction

This is one of a series of four studies which were undertaken to obtain a better understanding of why people have to struggle throughout their adult lives, in all countries and organisations, at all levels, to maintain and improve their standard of living and quality of life.

We know what people are struggling to achieve {3, 4} and so these studies explore why people have to struggle by looking at what they are struggling against.

The main report 'What People are Struggling Against' (See chapter 10) brings together the work reported in the four component studies by extracting and rearranging key findings from them.

To get an overview, it would be best to read the main report first. If you want more information on particular aspects of interest, you could then go to the component studies (See chapter 11, 12, 13, 14).

Understanding how Society is Organised

Ownership

Ownership {2, 8} is the right to possess something and to decide what is to be done with it. If I own something it belongs to me and I decide what is to be done with it. An example would be owning a house.

Possession is having something in one's custody as distinct from owning it. If I possess something it belongs to another but I can decide how to use it. An example would be renting a house.

Another example would be deciding what to do with my money (ownership) or deciding and controlling the use of money belonging to someone else (possession).

And considering the right to ownership, two questions need to be considered. Namely where does the right come from and how is it exercised.

The right to own property varies among societies. Ownership rights are based on man-made owner-serving laws and there has been little, if any, grassroots community-orientated participation in their drafting.

In other words, such man-made laws which assign ownership 'rights' to owners have been devised by the owners themselves or by those who serve them.

Ownership of land and means of production, of funds and wealth, has always been accumulated at someone else's expense. All belonged to the community, belonged to all alike. And the source of profit (surplus) is money which belongs to another, to someone else. Corporations, for example, are continually collecting money from the population, are enriching themselves by doing so, without acknowledging or returning corresponding ownership rights. <2>

A human right is something one may legally or morally claim, is the state of being entitled to a privilege or immunity or authority to act. Human rights are those held to be claimable by any living person, apply to all living people. Every living person is entitled to them.

So ownership of land and means of production, of funds and wealth, rightfully belongs to the community, belongs to all alike, is a human right. Those who have accumulated them have only possession, which means that they can use and apply them but may do so only on behalf of the community and that they are accountable to the community for the way in which they do so.

Limited Liability

According to owner-serving law, companies (corporations) are owned by people. People can buy shares, a share representing a small part of the company. The more shares they own, the greater is the part of the enterprise they own.

Owner-serving law lays down {7} that after owners have paid for their shares, they are not responsible for the company's debts to others such as suppliers, employees or customers.

Which means that owners take the profits but have transferred much of their risk to other people, to suppliers, customers, and employees.

What we see is a system where owners enrich themselves by using and risking other people's moneys.

Control and Power {2, 8}

Owner-serving laws enable shareholders to elect a board of directors, usually on the basis of one vote per share. So the majority shareholder decides who, apart from himself or his representative, is appointed to the board of directors. In this way he determines the policy of the enterprise.

Hence other shareholders usually have little say or interest in deciding policy or in managing the company. What is left for them to decide is whether to sell the shares they hold or whether to buy more.

So the person who is the majority shareholder <1> has in effect taken possession of the ownership rights of the other shareholders and can use the company's assets for his own ends.

He in effect controls the enterprise (organisation) and decides what is to be done and how it is to be done.

So the system is organised so that a few, a relatively very few, people at the top take the key decisions. Considering mergers and take-overs, we see them battling with each other for more power, for greater control, over people and resources.

Decision-making

Although a company does not make decisions it can be held responsible and can be held to account for decisions made by individuals within it. To that extent it serves as a cover for those who take make decisions, for owners and directors. {2, 8}

Income and Wealth

Directors are motivated by pay in its various forms, by greater wealth and by greater influence which includes dispensing patronage, and power. The pay of directors is what owners decide to pay themselves and their directors, is what the market will bear and increases with increasing influence and power. {3-4, 9}

The National Remuneration Pattern {5} is a precise pictorial record of the differentials within a country and between countries, from top to bottom, from young to old. It is used to assess changes in income and differentials for individuals, groups and professions. It also shows the relative value placed on different kinds of work. At the top are the owners or those who work directly for them, at the bottom are wage earners, pensioners, the poor.

What we see is a pattern of differentials which rewards service to the owners and their establishment rather than ability or service to the community. The nurse, the teacher, the fire-fighter and the police officer are at present paid comparatively little for the work they do.

In addition, purchasing power is being transferred from the bottom to the top. It is being transferred from those who can least afford to reduce their standard of living, to those at the other end to whom the extra purchasing power means greater luxury. The same percentage increase means a far greater amount at the top compared with the bottom of the income scale. In this way inflation is used to redistribute take-home purchasing power from the bottom to the top. Differentials and poverty increase even in an affluent society under full employment as long as attention continues to be focused on percentage increases instead of on amounts. {5}

It has been estimated {10} that 10 percent of the UK population were sinking into direct poverty, any gains in income being overtaken by the increasing cost of living. The next 20 percent were losing out, were being reduced to relative poverty. On the other hand the top 0.4 percent of the population took gains in take-home purchasing power which were 100 times those received by the general population. {5}

Community, Corporations and Profit Motivation

'Purpose of Any Enterprise' and 'Profit Motivation'

The purpose of any enterprise is to satisfy the community's needs by providing high quality goods and services at reasonable prices.

Those who can satisfy its needs are motivated by the community towards doing so by the reward, that is by the resulting profit. This process is referred to as 'profit motivation'. {6}

What matters is the value of the service to the community. Success is measured not by financial gain (profit) taken by owners, but by what the community gains.

The real profit or gain any enterprise achieves is the gain which the community obtains as a result of the enterprise's operations. Thus the social costs, that is costs to the community (such as pollution or unemployment) of any operation, have to be taken into account. {1}

For the free-market economic system to work, it is essential that prices are allowed to float unhindered according to the unhindered natural balance between supply and demand, within limits set to protect the community.

This means that there must be free unhindered competition.

It also means that profit margins and prices need to be controlled effectively so as to protect the community from exploitation. {6}

In this way the community attempts to ensure that its needs are satisfied at reasonable prices, that it gets good value for money.

Profit as Overriding or Sole Objective

Problems arise when profit becomes an overriding or sole objective to owners, directors or managers, and they concentrate on maximising profits regardless of cost to others, regardless of the cost and consequences to the community. Profits are then maximised regardless of the cost to the community, limited only by the likelihood of unpleasant consequences. {1}

Profits can be increased by reducing labour costs. Those wishing to increase profits regardless of the cost to others, will thus aim to reduce the standard of living of the working population, and will aim to increase the needs of the working population so that people will work for less. And putting the interest of the owners before that of the community is the main cause of our deteriorating environment and of our deteriorating quality of life. {1}

The report 'Social Responsibility, Profits and Social Accountability' {1} showed that we are faced with a sequence of incidents, disasters and catastrophes which are increasing in frequency and in severity, affecting more and more people. The consequences of such socially irresponsible behaviour are now such that they threaten the survival of people as human beings.

Capital and Wealth, Owners and Population

Shareholders would not even consider handing their moneys over to a corporation without in return becoming an owner of a corresponding part of the corporation, without getting a corresponding number of shares in return.

Customers are not given a choice. The corporation (its owners) simply take their customers' moneys

- for getting back money already spent on the business and
- for expanding the business

without giving the community corresponding ownership rights.

To 'rob' is to take unlawfully. But we are here looking at moneys being taken legally and largely without the owners' knowledge or agreement. What is taking place is perhaps best described by the phrase 'legalised robbery'.

Taking Moneys from Customers to Recover Money Already Spent on the Business

Money spent on new equipment and buildings is written off against income, say over a period of five years for equipment. After five years the enterprise has collected from its customers whatever has been spent on such assets. These moneys are deducted from income as a cost before calculating corporation (income) tax, in other words the enterprise pays no income tax on these amounts.

So an enterprise collects from its customers whatever its assets like equipment and buildings have cost, doing so without paying income tax on the amounts it collects.

And every time one buys goods or services, the price includes not only the manufacturer's and supplier's costs and profits, but also includes moneys (depreciation; capital replacement) for replacing their buildings and equipment.

Taking Moneys from Customers for Expanding the Business

As said already, no shareholder would simply hand his money over to a corporation (to its owners) without getting in return a corresponding share of the corporation's assets.

Yet when one buys goods or services, the price includes not only costs and profits, but also includes moneys which manufacturers and suppliers accumulate in 'reserves' for expanding the business or taking over other businesses.

So corporations (their owners) are continually collecting money from the population, are enriching themselves by doing so, without acknowledging or returning corresponding ownership rights.

Co-operatives and Mutual Aid Societies

Even co-operatives and mutual aid societies (building societies, credit unions) have been retaining some of their members' profits each year, for no apparent valid reason, accumulating these moneys for over 150 years <3>. By continually adding these moneys to their reserves they have become rich and powerful. That is, their chief executives and directors have become powerful, influential, and well paid. {2, 9, 11, 13}

And this explains some of the odd things which have been taking place such as

> Buyers of the Trustee Savings Bank receiving not only ownership of the bank but also the money they bought it with. {12}

> Lloyds Bank in effect using C&G Building Society's reserves to persuade C&G's members, both depositors and borrowers, into voting their mutual self-aid society out of existence. {9}

> Abbey National apparently using N&P Building Society's reserves to persuade N&P's members to hand over the society in return for share or cash payments drawn in effect mainly or completely from their own reserves, from their own capital. {9}

Who Benefits

These moneys are in effect taken from ordinary people and placed under the control of a few people at the top who in this way gain power, are enabled to dispense patronage (and support each other), gain high incomes and much wealth.

This 'legalised robbery' seems to be a key feature of the way society is organised to benefit those at the top.

Using Employees' Moneys to Gain Control over, and so Take Possession of, the Population's Wealth

Company pension funds generally offer better pension provisions than commercial pension schemes. At first employers used their pension schemes as a way of motivating people to stay with the employer, to reduce staff turnover and its associated expenses.

Company pension funds in the UK are usually managed by 'trustees' on behalf of the pension fund's contributors and pensioners. But the terms of the trust deed usually provide that the employer (the company) has a controlling say in how the fund's moneys are to be invested and used <4>. And some employers have insisted that pension fund surpluses be transferred to company profits.

Pension funds run into many GBP billions and between them own, and thus are in position to influence and control, much if not most of UK's equities.

These moneys and funds should be under the democratic control of those who contributed and those who are contributing to them. But ultimate control, and the power and influence that goes with it, have in effect been taken from the working population and placed in the hands of those who own and control companies (corporations).

Company credit unions provide some financial services to members and some company credit unions are very large indeed.

In the USA over 75 per cent of credit unions are run by employers who in this way control the lending and investing of over USD 151 billion. In the UK also there are credit unions run by employers for their employees. Whoever controls a credit union also controls its reserves. It seems as if here also the employer (company) may be gaining control over enormous capital sums.

Control of these moneys and funds should be under the democratic control of those who contributed and those who are contributing to them, should be in their hands and be exercised by them. But at present it appears that, although limited by certain legal safeguards, the employer, that is those at the top, have a deciding control over these moneys.

Notes and References

Notes

<1> Or the person who is the majority shareholder of the holding company in whose name the majority of the shares are registered

<2> See 'Capital and Wealth, Owners and Population'

<3> Since I discovered this and published my findings {2} there have been isolated instances of co-operatives moving in the direction of giving their members a better deal.

<4> There are legal safeguards which protect pension fund members to a considerable extent. For example, I remember one corporation which used its pension fund for providing subsidised mortgages to those managers it relocated. Subsidised by charging a below-market rate of interest. They stopped doing so after a member of staff pointed out that the pension fund had to obtain the best return it could for its members and so could not be used to subsidise staff relocations.

References

{ 1} Social Responsibility, Profits and Social Accountability.
Incidents, Disasters and Catastrophes.
The Worldwide Struggle for Social Accountability.
Community Aims and Community Leadership.
Manfred Davidmann, 1979, 1995
solhaam.org

{ 2} 'Cooperatives and Cooperation:
Causes of Failure, Guidelines for Success'
Manfred Davidmann
ISBN 978-0-85192-056-6

{ 3} In 'Management and Leadership:
Local, National, Multinational (Global),
Principles and Practice'
Manfred Davidmann
ISBN 978-0-85192-057-3
See chapter 4: 'Motivation'

{ 4} See chapter 16:
'The Will to Work: What People Struggle to Achieve'
Manfred Davidmann

{ 5} Work and Pay, Incomes and Differentials:
Employer, Employee and Community
Manfred Davidmann, 1981-1995, 2007
solhaam.org

{ 6} Community Economics: Principles
Manfred Davidmann, 1992, 1996
solhaam.org

{ 7} See chapter 3:
      'Ownership and Limited Liability'
      Manfred Davidmann

{ 8} See chapter 5,
      'Ownership and Deciding Policy: Companies,
      Shareholders, Directors and Community'
      Manfred Davidmann

{ 9} In 'Cooperatives and Cooperation:
      Causes of Failure, Guidelines for Success'
      Manfred Davidmann
      ISBN 978-0-85192-056-6
      See chapter 5.3: Building Societies

{10} Appropriate Pay
      Manfred Davidmann
      Social Organisation Ltd

{11} In 'Cooperatives and Cooperation:
      Causes of Failure, Guidelines for Success'
      Manfred Davidmann
      ISBN 978-0-85192-056-6
      See chapter 5.7: Mondragon Co-operatives
      (Mondragon Corporacion Cooperativa)

{12} In 'Cooperatives and Cooperation:
      Causes of Failure, Guidelines for Success'
      Manfred Davidmann
      ISBN 978-0-85192-056-6
      See chapter 5.1: The Trustee Savings Bank Give-
      Away

{13} In 'Cooperatives and Cooperation:
      Causes of Failure, Guidelines for Success'
      Manfred Davidmann
      ISBN 978-0-85192-056-6
      See chapter 5.2: Credit Unions

Chapter 13

Taxing the Population for Private Profit

Summary

This report shows how taxpayers' moneys are used in different ways to enlarge the profits of companies (corporations) and thus of their owners. Companies (corporations) are in effect allowed to tax the population and are also allowed to pass large parts of their operating costs to the taxpayers.

Moneys saved by spending less on social security for those in need and gained by collecting more tax from the working population, is apparently being used to reduce the taxes collected from the rich and from corporations.

Introduction

This is one of a series of four studies which were undertaken to obtain a better understanding of why people have to struggle throughout their adult lives, in all countries and organisations, at all levels, to maintain and improve their standard of living and quality of life.

We know what people are struggling to achieve {15, 16} and so these studies explore why people have to struggle by looking at what they are struggling against.

The main report 'What People are Struggling Against' (See chapter 10) brings together the work reported in the four component studies by extracting and rearranging key findings from them.

To get an overview, it would be best to read the main report first. If you want more information on particular aspects of interest, you could then go to the component studies (See chapter 11, 12, 13, 14).

Exporting Employment (Importing Unemployment) at Taxpayers' Expense

Corporations (Companies)

- Import goods and services which originate in low-wage countries, into a high-wage home country.
- Transfer manufacturing and service work from a high-wage home country to low wage countries.

The mark-up between buying or producing in a low-wage country, and then selling in a high-wage country, is often enormous <3>. Large additional profits result. Unemployment increases in the home country. There are many costs associated with unemployment such as social security payments to the newly unemployed. {5}

It is accepted as a principle of economics that social costs have to be paid by those causing them, so that the social costs of unemployment have to be paid by the enterprise which caused the unemployment in the first place {3}.

The different costs to individuals and community which result from unemployment are listed in Appendix 1. The social cost of unemployment to the community is the total cost to the community, is the sum of all the items listed there.

Companies, however, are not made to pay the resulting costs of unemployment, are allowed to pass these operating costs to the community and are thus making large profits at the expense of the community. {5}

In the UK, an individual was in 1998 reported to have been jailed for seven years for only threatening to contaminate a food if the producer did not pay him GBP 30,000 {7}. If he had carried out his threat the social costs would have been considerable and so he was jailed, presumably both as a punishment and to deter others from similar activities.

On the other hand, companies and corporations threaten to make people unemployed, and carry out these threats actually making hundreds and thousands of people unemployed with massive consequential social costs <1>. They also do so for the sake of private profit but no action is taken to prevent them from doing so by recovering the social costs from them, or to punish and deter by punitive sentencing.

All for the sake of profit, for personal gain of wealth, power, influence and control over others, for 'empire building'.

Taxing the Population to Benefit Corporations

A multinational company can minimise its liability for corporation tax by transfer pricing, that is by making book entries which transfer profits to the country with the lowest corporation tax. This tax avoidance is legal and governments have not legislated to prevent this practice. {4}

Say a multinational has increased its profits by tax avoidance. The government's income from taxation has decreased accordingly. As the government's expenses have not changed it must make up this shortfall elsewhere. Usually from its other taxpayers, say from its citizens. So its citizens pay more tax, the government can now spend the same amount as before, the multinational's profits have increased.

In other words, the multinational's increased profits arise from money which is in effect collected by the government by taxation from its taxpayers.

The multinational, and this means the owners and directors of the multinational, are thus in effect taxing the people and in this way increasing the multinational's profits and thus their own incomes and wealth.

Reducing Public Spending to Benefit the Rich

The government spends for the community the money it receives from the community, collecting it through taxation. Questions which need to be answered {9} are:

1. 'How much money has to be collected to provide for the community's needs?', including the level of social security and health services people need and would like to have.

2. 'Who contributes how much?' to see how the tax load is being shared among different income groups (including income from all sources).

3. Who ought to contribute more, and who less?

4. 'What effect will proposed changes have?' on the standard of living and quality of life of the different income groups.

'Appropriate Pay' {6} discusses such questions at some length, illustrating them by changes which took place in the United Kingdom over a period of ten years.

When owner-serving governments 'reduce income tax' for individuals and corporations, it is the rich who gain much, the working population hardly benefits. This becomes obvious when instead of looking at percentages one considers the purchasing power of the amounts. One then sees that the amounts contributed by the rich are being drastically reduced. The rich also gain much from other government policies which transfer moneys to them. And there are likely to be ways for tax avoidance (legal) and tax avoidance would be condoned. {9}

To claim in such circumstances that government expenditure on public services has to be cut so as to make ends meet, appears to be very one-sided.

In 1994, a British newspaper reported {10} that

> the Swedish Social Democrats looked like replacing the ruling right-wing coalition in the coming election. The Social Democrats policies included increasing taxes on income, capital gains, share dividends and wealth.

> Just before the election a newspaper article by the managing directors of four well-known companies 'was interpreted as an attack' on Social Democrat policies. A top-level owner-industrialist stated that his family might move some of its companies abroad 'unless the Swedish government made deep cuts in public expenditure'.

The economic policies of a British conservative government, for example, in effect reduced the tax the rich were paying and so reduced the contribution from the rich towards government expenditure. The conservative government then attempted to make ends meet by firstly collecting more money from the lower paid and from the poor by substantially increasing VAT (by 50%), and secondly by drastically cutting social services and social insurance payments and benefits including expenditure on education and on the health service. {1}

161

Such reductions seem to aim also at reducing the social security of the working population in areas such as unemployment benefit, health insurance payments, social security benefits such as supplementary payments, and pension rights. For example, it has been reported that in Britain's National Health Service the number of hospital beds has steadily declined over a considerable number of years while the number of admissions has increased. {2}

Channelling Taxpayers' Moneys into Private Profits

Employers should pay wages which will provide a good life for employees and their families. But the lower the wage paid, the higher the profit. And there will be employers who are more interested in their own profits than in the welfare of their employees.

Some employers may then pay wages which are so low that employees are forced to work long hours merely to survive. A government may then make up such wages with means-tested income support benefits to a poverty-existence level. Which is apparently what happened in the UK while minimum-wage requirements ceased to be applied.

In such ways taxpayers' moneys are used to subsidise the profits of companies (corporations), of their owners.

Taxpayers' moneys are also used to subsidise the profits of companies (corporations) when a government pays a subsidy to a company for every new employee. This is so regardless of whether the subsidy is paid as a single payment or whether it is paid for a limited period as part of the employee's wage.

Eton, a British establishment's exclusive 'public' boarding-school was, in 1997, reported to have about 1,260 pupils most of whom paid fees of about GBP 13,400 each year. Apparently nineteen of Britain's prime ministers were educated at Eton. The annual fee is close to the average annual British wage and Eton apparently had assets of about GBP 130 million without including buildings, 350 acres of grounds, and much else. {11}

But this wealthy and exclusive enterprise is registered as a charity. As far as I know this means that annual fees can be paid in accordance with a written covenant <4>, that is by stating in writing one's intention to make regular payments, which enables the college to recover the income tax paid on those sums and so reduce the level of fees.

And this means that the government, that is the working population, is subsidising Eton college by something like GBP 6 million each year. This figure is based on its income from fees alone and it appears to have additional 'investment income of millions'.

There are a considerable number of 'public' schools in the UK which appear to be almost exclusively educating a very small and rich section of the population.

Here taxpayers' moneys are in effect used to subsidise without means-testing the income and lifestyle of the parents. Can we afford to give away such large sums to benefit almost directly only a small number of people who are not in need?

Overall, the amounts channelled in such ways into private profits seem large. There may be investment grants, depreciation allowances, grants in aid, tax allowances, tax-free benefits, loans at favourable terms or other ways of financial support to various enterprises in industry, agriculture and the service sector. {9}

Very large amounts are apparently handed over yearly to increase the wealth and power of a small number of people without any corresponding return to the community. They are generally given without any obligation to repay, without a corresponding transfer of ownership and control to those who provided the money, to us. {9}

No banker, no financial institution, no shareholder would dream of giving away their capital without making sure of retaining ownership and control over this money, through the transfer of corresponding securities and ownership rights, and of direct and indirect participation in the resulting profits. {9}

So how come a democratically elected government can hand over public moneys to owners of companies (corporations) without getting corresponding ownership rights in return?

And how come public moneys can find their ways into private profits in such ways?

Condoning Tax Avoidance by the Rich

It has been reported {12-14} that the amount of assets hidden in Britain's offshore tax havens totals more than GBP 350 billion. Apparently companies and trusts are placed in tax havens to avoid paying taxes, appear to be asset-holding rather than trading. It seems they do not have to file proper public accounts nor do they need to reveal the identity of their directors, that is of those who own and control them.

The amount of tax lost to the British government from allowing tax-free status to these offshore islands has been estimated in the absence of reliable information as possibly being of the order of GBP 20 billion {13}, a large amount. One would like more comprehensive information but this estimate indicates a possibly staggering amount of tax-avoidance (legal) by those who are rich.

There would seem to be no good or valid reason for condoning tax-avoidance by those who are rich.

What stands out is that in such ways the rich are apparently allowed to avoid paying a fair share of the tax load. Condoning tax-avoidance increases the tax load on the working population.

We saw <2> that

> A multinational company can minimise its liability for corporation tax by transfer pricing {4}, that is by making book entries which transfer profits to the country with the lowest corporation tax.

A unitary taxation system can overcome this tax avoidance by assessing the actual profits being generated by a multinational in a particular country. American state governments have tried to install systems of unitary taxation but, as far as I know, multinational corporations have been able to dissuade state governments from applying such systems.

Studies published in the USA {8}, for example, tell us much about the extent to which multinationals can avoid paying tax on their profits. These present a disturbing picture. It seems that at times some top companies pay no federal income tax or obtain an overall rebate. Tax allowances appear to add well over USD 100 billion each year to the accounts of US corporations, and are thus given to owners and directors.

The ways in which taxation can be used to shift the tax load between income groups are numerous and often hide behind fine-sounding phrases.

Companies (corporations) have to distribute yearly a 'Funds Flow Statement' to their shareholders which states in plain language where moneys have come from, and what they have been spent on, for a particular year.

We should get similar independently audited statements from our government stating what moneys they have received and what these have been spent on. Stating in plain language who provides how much, for different income groups, showing types of taxes referred back to these income groups, and what the moneys have been spent on. Including and showing direct and indirect payments and transfers to the income groups, as well as showing what taxpayers received in return for the taxes collected from them.

And we should get a funds flow statement for the country's operations as a whole.

Appendix 1:   THE SOCIAL COSTS OF UNEMPLOYMENT

The social costs of unemployment {5} to people as individuals, to their families, and to the community as a whole, are {5}:

Individuals

Poverty, lack of spending money

Frustration, despair

Young people without full-time work experience

Social disillusionment

Ill health

Reduced life span

Mental illness

Increasing suicide rate

Drug abuse, crime

Families

Increased family breakup

Homelessness

Domestic violence

Community

Higher and rising crime rates

Brutalisation of lifestyle

Lost Income:

(1) Loss of income tax from those now unemployed.

(2) Loss of National Insurance contributions which would have been received from both employees and employers.

(3) Loss of Value Added Tax as the unemployed reduce their spending.

Increased Expenditure

>   (4) Increased cost of Unemployment Benefit (Among developed countries, the British rate of benefit appears to be one of the lowest).

>   (5) Increased cost of Social Security support payments.

>   (6) Increased costs for Health Service, Police and Prisons.

Note that persistent lack of care and consideration towards its members leads to a view of society as being hostile and unrewarding {15}. We now see this taking place and see its effects.

The social cost of unemployment to the community is the total cost to the community, is the sum of all the items listed here.

Notes and References

Notes

<1> See 'Appendix 1'

<2> See 'Taxing the Population to Benefit Corporations'

<3> Costs + Profit = Price

'Mark-up' is 'Profit' expressed as a percentage of 'Costs'

Say   Costs = 100
       Profit = 10

Then   Price = 100+10=110

And   Mark-up = (10/100)*100 = 10 percent

'Costs' include wages and salaries

<4> A 'covenant' in this context is a written agreement to make regular payments.

References

{ 1} Social Responsibility, Profits and Social
Accountability.
Incidents, Disasters and Catastrophes.
The Worldwide Struggle for Social Accountability.
Community Aims and Community Leadership.
Manfred Davidmann, 1979, 1995
solhaam.org

{ 2} In 'Management and Leadership:
Local, National, Multinational (Global),
Principles and Practice'
Manfred Davidmann
ISBN 978-0-85192-057-3
See chapter 2: 'Style of Management and
Leadership'

{ 3} Community Economics: Principles
Manfred Davidmann, 1992, 1996
solhaam.org

{ 4} See chapter 8:
'Transfer Pricing and Taxation'
Manfred Davidmann

{ 5} See chapter 7,
'Exporting and Importing of Employment and
Unemployment'
Manfred Davidmann

{ 6} Appropriate Pay
Manfred Davidmann
Social Organisation Ltd

{ 7} Seven years for dairy blackmail
Helen Carter
Guardian, 12/09/98

{ 8} The Resurgence of Business Investment & Corporate
Income Taxes
Citizens for Tax Justice, 1989
Robert S McIntyre, Douglas Kelly, Bruce L Fisher,
David Wilhelm, Helen Luce Dorrier

{ 9} In 'Management and Leadership:
Local, National, Multinational (Global),
Principles and Practice'
Manfred Davidmann
ISBN 978-0-85192-057-3
See chapter 9: 'Inflation, Balance of Payments and
Currency Exchange Rates'
which also discusses how base (general) interest
rates affect share prices and pensions, and the
struggle for a bigger share.

{10} Swedish chainsaw massacre
Greg McIvor
Guardian, 16/09/94

{11} How Eton entered the Kwik-Fit league
Clara Longrigg and John Carvel
Guardian, 21/04/97

{12} Billions hidden offshore
David Leigh
Guardian, 26/09/98

{13} Raid the tax havens
Guardian, 26/09/98

{14} Island tax havens face crackdown
Alan Travis
Guardian, 20/11/98

{15} In 'Management and Leadership:
Local, National, Multinational (Global),
Principles and Practice'
Manfred Davidmann
ISBN 978-0-85192-057-3
See chapter 4: 'Motivation'

{16} See chapter 16:
'The Will to Work: What People Struggle to Achieve'
Manfred Davidmann

Chapter 14

Corrupted Economics and Misguided (Misleading) Experts

Summary

This report shows how 'Economics' is used to misinform and mislead the general public, and looks at the role and vested interests of experts.

So this report discusses the relevance and reliability of some economic relationships, clearly stating them and the underlying considerations as well as commenting on misleading political interpretations and misuses of the work of economists.

Subjects discussed include the cost of living, the fight against inflation, index linking, unemployment, uses of the base interest rate, share prices, currency exchange rates, the role and vested interests of experts.

Introduction

This is one of a series of four studies which were undertaken to obtain a better understanding of why people have to struggle throughout their adult lives, in all countries and organisations, at all levels, to maintain and improve their standard of living and quality of life.

We know what people are struggling to achieve {2, 16} and so these studies explore why people have to struggle by looking at what they are struggling against.

The main report 'What People are Struggling Against' See chapter 10) brings together the work reported in the four component studies by extracting and rearranging key findings from them.

To get an overview, it would be best to read the main report first. If you want more information on particular aspects of interest, you could then go to the component studies (See chapter 11, 12, 13, 14).

Inflation - Inflation-proof Profits – Struggle for Cost-of-living Increases

When prices of imported goods increase or wages go up, costs increase. Profit is commonly marked-up <2> at a fixed percentage of cost. As costs increase, profits increase automatically.

These profits are paid to shareholders by way of dividends and as capital gains. Part of the profits are paid out as dividends which are annual cash payments. The remaining profits are retained in the enterprise and increase the value of its shares. The shareholder realises this capital gain when selling his shares.

Inflation is an increase in prices, in the cost-of-living. Inflation increases costs. Profits increase correspondingly and automatically. All the profits are given to shareholders by way of dividends and capital gains.

The higher prices are felt by wage and salary earners who demand pay increases in line with increasing prices, in line with the increasing cost of living. Prices increase as a result, the increase depending both on the extent to which wage and salary demands are satisfied and on how much of the price consists of labour costs. {12}

So costs increase, profits increase automatically, prices increase, employees struggle to keep up, wages increase,

so costs increase, profits increase automatically, prices increase, employees struggle to keep up, wages increase,

so costs increase, ...

It does not really matter where you enter the upward spiral to tell the story. Start with wages going up and 'wage inflation' looks like the cause. Start with profits going up and increasing prices ('price inflation') looks like the cause.

So as prices increase, profits increase correspondingly and automatically and are given to shareholders. Wages and salaries increase only after employees struggle to maintain the purchasing power of their take-home pay and then only to the extent to which their demands are satisfied.

Misleading the Population

In this report we are looking at what seem to be misleading fictions and smokescreens in the field of economics which relate to exploiting people at work, as citizens, and in the market place.

What is being commented on is not the work of economists who are exploring and applying underlying relationships to the best of their knowledge and experience. The comments made here relate to work and pronouncements which appear to be biased by political ideology, which appear to be misleading political interpretations and misuses of the work of economists.

Inflation and Cost of Living

Consider this example:

> The UK's RPI (Retail Price Index) measures changes in the cost of living of a typical household. Its component items and their weighting are based on population consumption surveys and representative sampling. This is the cost of living index which measures changes in the cost of living and it does its job well.
>
> If the RPI were called the 'cost of living' index, it would tell ordinary citizens that this was an easily understood measure of how changes in prices and government policies were affecting them. It would point to its use for negotiating cost-of-living pay increases.

But another index (RPIX) was then introduced by a conservative (Tory) government which excluded mortgage interest payments. In the UK the purchase of one's own home by taking out a mortgage is widespread. Mortgage interest costs depend on the level of the centrally determined base interest rate and so this index does not reflect the corresponding increases in the cost of living when the base interest rate is increased.

Still another index (RPIY) was then introduced which excluded not only mortgage interest payments but also excluded indirect taxes which had to be paid by all regardless of how small their income. It excludes VAT (Value Added tax), Council tax (local government tax), excise duty, car purchase tax, insurance and airport tax. In other words, this index does not show the effects on a typical household's cost of living when such taxes are introduced or increased.

The RPI index is a good cost of living index but instead of being called 'cost of living index' it is called 'Headline rate of inflation'. The RPIX index is called 'Underlying rate of inflation'. To me these are misleading terms which confuse instead of illuminate, and which seem intended to confuse.

Such misleading developments are particularly harmful because we have, and have had for many years, the knowledge, understanding and means for automatically increasing pay and pensions in line with the cost of living (inflation), allowing at the same time for increased merit (knowledge and experience) and the betterment (share of increased national income) {4, 9}. Index linking is one aspect of this process and index linking is discussed in more detail in the next section.

Index Linking

Consider how index linking operates in relation to the increasing cost of living. {9}

Owners' profits (dividends plus capital gain) increase automatically whenever costs increase. So profits are in effect linked to costs, to inflation.

Linking of pay to a cost of living index takes the heat out of employer and employee pay bargaining, reduces confrontation and strife, eliminates having to struggle just to maintain one's place. It is at times applied to essential public services such as medical, fire, police, teaching and government. {9}

Pay is reviewed at intervals and is increased according to changes in the index. If the index has increased by 2 per cent say, then pay is increased by 2 per cent. Another way of linking is to increase pay by a given percentage whenever the index has increased by that percentage. {9}

But the cost of living index should reliably reflect the cost of living of the working population, by its composition and weighting, and be protected against politically motivated change which favours one side or the other. {9}

For example the index needs to be protected against misleading changes of the kind which try to replace a validly compiled, appropriate and easily understood 'cost-of-living' index with something else.

After index linking, pay bargaining can concentrate on the main issue, namely on how to share out the increased value created by the joint effort of both sides, and on how to adjust national differentials to ensure that no one section gains unfairly at the expense of others and to balance out inequalities. {9}

A ruling establishment could be expected to avoid and resist index-linking of pay because index-linking would limit their efforts to increase profits by lowering the standard of living of the population. But what stands out is the way the UK's trade union and Labour party establishments appear to have neglected index-linking for so many years.

The 'Fight against Inflation'

While profits, dividends and 'capital gains' increase automatically, a bitter struggle develops as owners and employers attempt to use inflation as an excuse for reducing labour costs, that is wage rates, wages and salaries of the working population, so as to increase profits still further. Employees are then not compensated for increased skill, experience and responsibility (increased merit), do not receive their share of the increasing national income and wealth (the betterment), do not receive merit increases and betterment increases. {4}

Pensioners also stand to lose betterment increases, do not receive their share of the increasing national income and wealth (the betterment) which is being achieved on the basis of their past labours. {4}

Changes in the cost of living are measured by the cost-of-living index (RPI). The betterment is the extent to which increases in average earnings exceed increases in the cost-of-living. {4}

Here is an example. Since 1980 the UKs Tory government has withheld from pensioners their share of the increasing national income and wealth, for no apparent good reason, amounting to something like 2 percent of their pension every year. Pensions had been linked to the index of average earnings but in 1980 they were linked to the cost-of-living index. As a result their present pensions are a fraction of what they ought to be, have now to be increased by 34 percent just to reach the level at which they should be now. And pensioners still have to be compensated for the moneys withheld from them without good reason by the government since 1980.

This attack on the living standards of the working population is misleadingly called a 'fight (or battle) against inflation' to persuade the working population to tighten its belts, to reduce its standard of living.

In Britain, for example {1}

> A salary and wages 'freeze' by a Labour government did not restrict dividends.

> A Labour government limited wage increases to 5 percent maximum at a time when inflation was running at roughly 10 percent p.a.

The so-called 'fight against inflation' appears to be an economic deception designed to exploit the working population even further. Just how one-sided this is can be judged by the fight supposedly being against 'wage inflation'. Left out of consideration are excessive price increases, profits, dividends or capital gains. Also more or less ignored is the large top-level remuneration which has been increasing yearly for some years at up to four or five times the rate of inflation, increasing each year by amounts many times exceeding the average income of the working population.

In the USA, 'Citizens for Tax Justice' in 1991 published a revealing article 'The total cost of the wealthy's tax cuts explains the entire increase in the federal budget deficit!' {10}

In the UK {14}

> 'The best-paid directors in the country's largest companies received increases that were six times the rate of inflation and four times the growth in average earnings, ...'

> 'In the early 1990s ... corporate bosses were indulging themselves with pay rises of 25 to 30 per cent ...'

> 'The highest-paid directors now collect as much in a working week as the average employee earns in a year.'

And {15}

> 'Over the past 10 years, the remuneration of the highest-paid directors has risen at three times the rate of the wider workforce.'

Inflation and Unemployment

I consider correlations of unemployment and inflation rates to be largely spurious and inconsistent, apparently depending on time and place, on how unemployment and inflation are defined, apparently not taking into account all relevant factors.

Consider this argument. Say unemployment is low and labour is in demand. 'Free enterprise' competition for labour causes wage rates to increase. Increasing wage rates cause inflation.

The argument then goes that one is fighting against inflation, that falling unemployment causes inflation so that to keep inflation down one has to increase unemployment or at least keep it above a certain level.

In other words, one is supposed to keep unemployment up, or increase it, so as to prevent free-market competition for labour pushing wages up as this would reduce profits.

This piece of logical-seeming misleading argument is based on the untrue assumption that inflation is caused only by wage increases.

Conveniently ignored by those putting forward such misleading arguments are all the other causes and relevant considerations mentioned in different places in this report including the effect of a country's balance of payments and consequent economic policies on the exchange rate and the purchasing power of its currency.

General Interest Rates: Unemployment, Profits and Share Prices

We hear about the effect of changes in the bank rate, in the general interest rate, on unemployment and deflation. I consider that such relationships, if they exists at all, are at best remote and theoretical, have not been proved conclusively either way. As regards such matters, however, what I am doing here is to discuss only selected aspects.

An increase in general interest rates increases profits for lenders (within a country and internationally). It also increases costs for borrowers and thus inflation, but only to the extent to which loan interest plays a part in the costs. So profits increase in greater measure than costs or inflation.

Money moves towards a better investment. If interest-paying investments give a better return than dividend-paying shares, people will buy interest-paying investments and sell their shares. Interest-paying investments are then in demand and their prices increase, shares are not in demand and their prices drop. Share prices will continue to drop until the amount of the dividend payment (in currency units such as USD) represents a return <3> from the share which is the same as the interest paid by interest-paying investments.

So increasing the general interest rate reduces share prices, reducing the general interest rate increases share prices. And the return from shares (dividend payment as a percentage of share price) tends to move towards the new interest rates. As follows:

Price of share	(USD)	100	
Return from share <3>	(%)	5	
Dividend received	(USD)	5	
General interest rate	(%)	5	
New general interest rate	(%)	8	2
Dividend received (No change)	(USD)	5	5
New return from share (matches interest)	(%)	8	2
New price of share	(USD)	62.5	250

This sample calculation illustrates the effect. However, share prices also depend on other factors such as the risk associated with the investment and the country's creditworthiness as reflected in currency exchange rates.

Other key uses of general interest rate in relation to balance of payments and currency exchange rates are discussed in the following section.

Balance of Payments - Currency Exchange Rates - General Interest Rates - Inflation - Devaluation Profiteering. {12}

Suppose our country spends more on imports than it earns from exports. We then see a payments deficit which has to be made good as imports have to be paid for. We pay from our foreign currency reserves. <1>

If the payments deficit persists and we are using up too much of our foreign currency reserves we can increase the amount of foreign currency deposited with us by increasing the interest paid by us to depositors. This is a form of short-term borrowing.

What attracts deposits is the relative interest rate. If another country offers more, that is where the deposits are likely to go. So what we are doing is to attract more deposits by increasing our interest rate in relation to that of others. And we adjust our interest rate when other countries change theirs.

Interest rates affect the cost of borrowing and the profit from lending. So increasing interest rates increase prices, increase the cost of living.

The value of our currency depends on the assets backing it and on the amount of money in circulation. These assets include the foreign currency reserves. As the reserves drop so does the value of the currency as each currency unit is then backed by fewer assets. Our currency becomes weaker compared with other currencies.

Instead of increasing the interest rate we can pay our debts by printing more money. This increases the amount of money in circulation. As our assets have remained unchanged, each currency unit is now backed by fewer assets. The value of each currency unit decreases accordingly and our currency weakens relative to other currencies.

When we do not make ends meet we become less credit-worthy, our currency weakens and so does its purchasing power. It buys less and prices increase.

As our currency weakens (devalues) so our exports become cheaper abroad but we have to pay more for imports. This reduces our standard of living relative to others abroad as they find our produce cheaper while we find theirs more expensive.

We now have to produce and sell a greater volume of exports so as to earn as much foreign currency as we did before and have to sell even more if we are to improve our position, if we are to benefit from the devaluation.

Only too often do producers and exporters charge abroad what the market will bear, charging the highest price their goods will fetch, without reducing prices when their currency is devalued. The result is that the producer's and exporter's profits increase enormously because they sell the same volume as before but make a far greater profit on each sale.

We saw that as our currency weakens (devalues) so our standard of living is reduced relative to others abroad. So these greater profits are made at the expense of a general lowering of the standard of living of the country as a whole. And as prices have not been lowered, there is no corresponding gain in the volume of production, that is in economic growth. And the greatly increased profit redistributes income and wealth from the general population whose standard of living is falling, distributing it to those at the top who benefit from such profit increases.

Maximising Profits: What the Market Will Bear: Price Profiteering

In practice directors are generally required by owner-serving laws to act first and foremost in the interests of the owners, so that it is profit which is maximised. Short-term and long-term profits can be and are being maximised regardless of the cost to others, that is regardless of the cost to the community. {5}

Profits are maximised regardless of the cost to the community, limited only by the likelihood of unpleasant consequences such as restraining fines, punitive legal punishment or adverse publicity. {1, 5}

The mark-up between buying or producing in a low-wage country, and then selling in a high-wage country, is often enormous. Large additional profits result at the cost of increasing unemployment in the high-wage country. {7}

Imports are priced at what the market will bear, or just under {7}. The enormous profit margins then cause production to move from high-wage to low-wage countries. The consequence is a lowering of standard of living in high-wage countries to that in low-wage countries, instead of a raising of standard of living in low-wage countries to that in high wage countries.

The phrase 'the polluter pays' sums up popular feeling about how to right past wrongs, about how to hold to account those whose profits are made at the expense of the community and those who benefit from antisocial activities. {5}

178

It appears that fines imposed for antisocial company behaviour are usually too small to be an effective deterrent, bearing in mind that prices are what the market will bear and the small chance of the company being found out or taken to court.

And it is the customer who is made to pay because enterprises recover any cleaning-up costs and compensation payments by increasing their prices. {5}

So it is the customer who pays while the company is unlikely to be deterred from socially irresponsible behaviour by fines which in amount are ridiculously small compared with the size of the company's overall operations. {5}

One of the most effective restraints has been found to be the fear of bad publicity, of public awareness of socially irresponsible company behaviour, with its effect on company image, consumer trust and market share, and thus on profits. Particularly so when publicity names those responsible for making anti-social decisions within the company or for condoning and omitting to restrain the company's anti-social activities.

To owners and employers the worth of a job is what has to be paid to get it done. They want work to be done at the lowest rate at which they can get it done {4, 6} as profits can be increased by reducing labour costs, by exploiting employees.

So owners and employers will, when they can, pressurise the working population into accepting even lower rates of pay by increasing the working population's needs {1-3}. Doing so by advocating greater unemployment, reducing social security, reducing national health service provisions, weakening the quality of education (knowledge, clear thinking, understanding, objective evaluation).

So profits are apparently being maximised regardless of the cost to others, to the community. Without care or concern for the condition, standard of living or quality of life of the working population. Without being concerned about the in sum-total enormous human suffering which results.

Overall, what we see are consequences of decisions made at the top, and the results of putting them into effect. Results and consequences which at times make the decisions seem so brutal that they appear inhuman.

Role of Experts

An expert is a person having special knowledge or skill in a particular subject. Experts inform and advise and it would be better to refer to them as advisers.

We are here looking at the functional relationship between on the one hand the person who has to take the decision and on the other hand the advising expert. {11}

Within an organisation

> The adviser is accountable to his manager for giving expert advice and for the quality of his advice. {11}

> A person making a decision is accountable to his manager for the consequences of the decision he takes. Which includes that he is responsible, that is accountable, for obtaining expert advice, for accepting or rejecting this while clearly stating reasons, and for reporting useful results to the adviser. {11}

In a democracy,

> Experts inform and advise the electorate about what should, can or cannot be done and about likely consequences either way.

> The electorate, the population, decide what is to be done and by when it is to be done. The elected representative puts into effect the decisions made by the electors, that is policy set by the electors.

Note that people are not told what they must do. The role of experts is to advise.

An expert is supposed to advise to the best of his ability, knowledge, skill and experience and is responsible, that is accountable, for the quality of his advice. Responsible, that is accountable, also to those he is advising for the quality of his advice from their point of view, for the extent to which he is considering their best interests.

Too often do experts tell people what the expert thinks is good for the people to do. Too often it is the expert who decides or who attempts to compel others to do as told.

The difference it can make when experts restrict themselves to advising, pointing out what can and cannot be done, is enormous. This is clearly illustrated in a TV documentary about providing housing for people from inner city areas. The documentary clearly describes and illustrates the whole process, showing how architects acting as advisers can be instrumental in providing modern working-population housing described by one resident as 'heaven on earth'. {13}

Vested Interests of Experts

People assume that an expert who talks convincingly and seems sure of himself knows what he is talking about, an additional factor being that he is likely to use long important-sounding words with an air of conviction and certainty. This applies particularly in the areas of economics, psychology, sociology, philosophy and politics. {1}

'He who pays the piper may call the tune' is an old proverb which seems to describe rather well what is often seen in practice.

Employers are likely to pay close attention to what their employees say in public and particularly so when the occasion is in the public eye, is likely to be opinion-forming. Employees are aware of this, are likely to see such occasions as potentially career-advancing, are likely to be saying what employers would wish to hear. And so employers have a strong influence on what their employees say in public and employees are likely to be advocating viewpoints which are employer-serving instead of being people-serving and community-serving.

Bias is increased further because employers are likely to promote, and to put forward for making public statements, only those who agree with the employers' point of view.

And bias can be increased even further when media present mainly one point of view, say that of employers, or of a particular political party, or of advertisers.

Similarly, would it not be a good idea for each member of a government, each elected representative, to state in public what they personally are likely to gain, or lose, from the way they are voting on a particular legislation.

I feel that lists of such gains and losses may make interesting reading, for example about the recent changes by a conservative government to UKs local government taxation, from 'Council rate' (depending on property value) to Poll Tax (depending on number of resident people, on size of family) to Council Tax (Poll Tax amended because of public protest).

What people need to do is to consider the community's short-term and long-term interests objectively, seeing things as they are {8}, without bias. {1}

Notes and References

Notes

<1> Not considering here making ends meet by selling gold from our reserve, or selling of other assets, or long-term borrowing.

<2> Costs + Profit = Price

'Mark-up' is 'Profit' expressed as a percentage of 'Costs'

Say   Costs = 100
        Profit = 10

Then   Price = 100+10=110

And   Mark-up = (10/100)*100 = 10 percent

'Costs' include wages and salaries

<3> Return: Dividend payment expressed as a percentage of the price

References

{ 1}   Social Responsibility, Profits and Social Accountability.
        Incidents, Disasters and Catastrophes.
        The Worldwide Struggle for Social Accountability.
        Community Aims and Community Leadership.
        Manfred Davidmann, 1979, 1995
        solhaam.org

{ 2}   See chapter 16:
        'The Will to Work: What People Struggle to Achieve'
        Manfred Davidmann

{ 3}   In 'Management and Leadership:
Local, National, Multinational (Global),
Principles and Practice'
Manfred Davidmann
ISBN 978-0-85192-057-3
See chapter 2: 'Style of Management and
Leadership'

{ 4}   Work and Pay, Incomes and Differentials:
Employer, Employee and Community
Manfred Davidmann, 1981-1995, 2007
solhaam.org

{ 5}   Community Economics: Principles
Manfred Davidmann, 1992, 1996
solhaam.org

{ 6}   See chapter 5,
'Ownership and Deciding Policy: Companies,
Shareholders, Directors and Community'
Manfred Davidmann

{ 7}   See chapter 7,
'Exporting and Importing of Employment and
Unemployment'
Manfred Davidmann

{ 8}   See chapter 15:
'Using Words to Communicate Effectively'
Manfred Davidmann

{ 9}   The Right to Strike
Manfred Davidmann, 1996
solhaam.org

{10}   Inequality & The Federal Budget Deficit
Citizens for Tax Justice
Robert S McIntyre, 1991

{11}   In 'Management and Leadership:
Local, National, Multinational (Global),
Principles and Practice'
Manfred Davidmann
ISBN 978-0-85192-057-3
See chapter 6: 'Organising'

{12}   In 'Management and Leadership:
       Local, National, Multinational (Global),
       Principles and Practice'
       Manfred Davidmann
       ISBN 978-0-85192-057-3
       See chapter 9: 'Inflation, Balance of Payments and
       Currency Exchange Rates'
       which also discusses how base (general) interest
       rates affect share prices and pensions, and the
       struggle for a bigger share.

{13}   TV Documentary on architecture and housing
       co-operatives
       Produced by Suzanne Davies, 1986
       Broadcast 06/06/98 in UK

{14}   The boardroom bonanza
       Lisa Buckingham and Roger Cowe
       Guardian, 22/07/98

{15}   Pleas for restraint fail to curb
       Lisa Buckingham and Roger Cowe
       Guardian, 22/07/98

{16}   In 'Management and Leadership:
       Local, National, Multinational (Global),
       Principles and Practice'
       Manfred Davidmann
       ISBN 978-0-85192-057-3
       See chapter 4: 'Motivation'

Chapter 15

Using Words to Communicate Effectively

Summary

Shows how to communicate more effectively, covering aspects of thinking, writing, speaking and listening as well as formal and informal communications.

Consists of guidelines found useful by university students and practising middle and senior managers.

Communicating with Words

Communication is the transmission of meaning to others.

Important is that 'meaning' is transferred. In other words, it is important the other persons understand what we want them to understand, that they understand the intended meaning.

More precisely, purposeful communication is the transmission of intended meaning to others.

Implied is

1. that the sender of the communication has clear knowledge and understanding of the meaning he wishes to convey, and

2. that the receiver interprets the message in such a manner that he receives the intended meaning.

Hence for effective communication the sender must determine the purpose of the communication and use words which have the same meaning for sender and receiver.

Meaning of Words

The scientific study of meaning is called Semantics.

Words and Labels

Words are labels. Labels are arbitrary.

Most common cause of misunderstanding arises from assuming that the word (a label) is the object. Two people can then be arguing about a concept, referring to it by using the same word, arguing because this word means something different to each of them.

So to be meaningful, words must establish the same thought (reference) in both the sender and receiver of a communication.

Words vary considerably as regards their value for communication. They differ in their level of abstraction. The greater the level of abstraction, the less meaning do they have.

Levels of Abstraction

1 Objects

Objects represent a relatively low level of abstraction as they can be seen and touched and their characteristics detailed accurately.

Here words are labels for objects such as table or chair.

2 Events

In addition to objects, both action and time are implied, and so these are more complex.

Examples are: Accident, sale, party.

3 Generalisations

Words are also used as labels for groups and collections of objects or events. These generalisations are more abstract and less precise.

Examples of such labels are: Furniture, machine tools, employees, parents.

Employees, for example, can be full-time, part-time, shift working, office working, home working, male, female, young, old, single, married, unskilled, skilled, professional, and more.

4 Value Judgements or Ideology

Value judgements and ideology are at the highest level of abstraction and words used as labels for them are quite useless for effective communication until the meaning of the word used is clearly defined in detail.

Examples of such labels are: Beautiful, valuable, necessary, luxury, lazy, free enterprise, truth.

Such words can be strung together and mixed with generalisations to provide good-sounding speeches and statements of the kind politicians like to use, to provide speeches and statements with no real meaning attached to the words used. Listeners or readers use their own idea of what the words mean and so their understanding of what is being said differs widely from person to person.

I listed the word 'truth' as an example of a label for a meaningless abstraction. Surely 'truth' ought to be more than a meaningless value judgement, so let us look at this in more detail.

Consider two media reports of a current event. Each reports the same event, each apparently telling the truth, each report giving its viewers different impressions of what actually happened.

How come? Can there be more than one truth?

Such reports may tell only part of what happened, may report only what seems relevant to the reporter, may then be selecting what seems to support the particular viewpoint of those who prepared the report.

Compare these 'truths' with that demanded from a witness in a court of law: 'The truth, the whole truth and nothing but the truth.'

Which means that what is required in a court of law is the truth with nothing taken away and nothing added.

If we agree on this as a definition, then the word 'truth' has become more meaningful.

Formal and Informal Communications

A distinction needs to be made between formal and informal communications. Formal communication implies that a record is kept, that what has been said or written can be attributed to its originator.

On the whole, written communications are formal. But statements may be qualified by phrases such as 'preliminary thoughts are ...'.

Oral (spoken) communication consists of direct or transmitted speech between two or more people. Oral communications are more likely to be misinterpreted than written ones, were regarded as informal but are now often recorded and treated as formal. Missing from such recordings is the body language consisting of facial expressions and gestures.

Consider an informal chat by telephone getting comments on matters of joint concern before producing a final report. Important is the possibility of a two-way flow of information, of immediate feedback, of a frank unreserved exchange of information, opinions and ideas.

The informal nature of such exploratory conversations is often ignored. People's preliminary thoughts can then be quoted against them as if they had been fully considered.

Although an answering (recording) machine ought to bleep at regular intervals while recording, conversations can be recorded in different ways by one person without the other being aware of this.

Hence one needs to make sure the other person is aware of the informal nature of the conversation. In other words, that the other person knows the conversation is not to be recorded and that the information is to be regarded as confidential until the matter has been fully considered.

There are, however, many formal oral communications, such as selection, grievance or appraisal interviews, or when negotiating. Characteristic is that a record is kept by those participating.

Rumours are hearsay. One person tells the next who tells another, and so on. But there are personal barriers as people tend to keep back, elaborate or enhance information in accordance with their likes and dislikes. Hence information tends to change in emphasis and content as it is passed from person to person. This makes rumours so unreliable a source of information.

Improving Communication

1. Clarify your own ideas before attempting to communicate them.

2. Be clear about the purpose of the communication. For example, its purpose could be to inform others, to obtain information or to initiate action.

3. See if the other person can repeat what you have said, in his or her own words.

Effective communication, however, depends also on attentive listening.

Effective Listening

Do not jump to conclusions before hearing what the other person has to say, and do not interrupt.

Interrupting prevents effective and meaningful communication, can prevent the speaker from making a valid point. Think how you would feel if you were interrupted just before making your key point.

It is up to the sender (originator) of the communication to use words which have the same meaning also for the receiver, for the listener. To ensure that you have understood the communication (message) correctly, you can repeat it in your own words to the other person.

For example, after being told how to get to a particular street one can ask "You mean, take the second street on the left?". Answers like "Yes, it is" or "Take the third on the left" confirm or improve our understanding of what we had been told.

And so, for effective listening:

1. Avoid jumping to conclusions, avoid making value judgements such as good or bad, desirable or undesirable, true or false, while the speaker is talking.

2. Listen to the full story.

3. Restate the other person's position in your own words.

Letters and Reports

1. Avoid slogans, catchwords (buzz-words), jargon.

   Use words or phrases which you could use naturally in conversation. Exceptions are technical terms and abbreviations which your reader will understand.

2. Use simple words and few of them.

3. Keep paragraphs and sentences short.

4. In-house e-mail is fast. Copies are readily distributed to all those interested and reach their destination almost immediately.

   Fast method for causing chaos as mistakes spread rapidly. Effects snowball as others act quickly using the mistaken information.

   Better to prepare draft replies but only post the replies after some hours, which allows considering, validating, completing and improving the draft.

Traps to Avoid

1. Avoid being blinded by words or phrases which sound good, expert, impressive, plausible or likely. Ask for a definition or explanation to be given in clear, simple, meaningful language.

2. Avoid being misled by illogical arguments, misleading publicity or propaganda.

   When propaganda is logical, and seen to be logical, it is difficult to argue against, to counter. Such propaganda is usually misleading because it is the premise, the first argument or underlying assumption, which misleads.

   In other words, a logical argument can be based on false assumptions or misleading information.

Chapter 16

The Will to Work: What People Struggle to Achieve

Summary

Community Leadership and Management
What People Struggle to Achieve
The Will to Work
Remuneration, Job Satisfaction, Motivation
Struggle for Independence and Good Life

Manfred Davidmann here clearly defines and describes motivation, its basis and 'motivating'.

Starting by considering motivation from the point of view of the employer (productivity, remuneration, job satisfaction), this leads to considering what people want and what they struggle to achieve.

A key part of the report is community orientated, including a detailed step-by-step listing of what people are struggling to achieve, their needs and wants, their achievements and objectives. This progression shows underdeveloped and developed people as they are, human beings at different stages of an identical struggle for a better life against those who wish to profit from their condition.

And you can assess how far the country/community you are living in has advanced in this struggle for independence and a good life for all, or where you are yourself on this scale.

Highlights are Figure 1 (Motivation of Directors) and Figure 3 (People's Needs and Wants, Achievements and Objectives: The Struggle for Independence and a Good Life).

The Will to Work

What one would like to do is to create a working environment in which people like working and in which people work well, a working environment which helps to enrich the life of those who work. One would like to satisfy the requirements of those who work and of those who employ as well as the requirements of the community as a whole.

It could be that 'motivating' seems such a complicated subject because it deals with people and people are all different. But when people are all different then the one thing they have in common is that they are all different and that is a good starting point.

Much has been written about motivation. When determining the motivation of those who direct in the United Kingdom it seemed to take as long to read up on the background of what is commonly called 'motivation' and summarise it in a few short paragraphs {1} as it took to carry out the rest of the investigation.

'Motivation' views the commitment of the individual to work and to his workplace from the point of view of factors originating within himself, from the point of view of individual needs, likes and preferences.

But one cannot talk about 'motivation' or 'motivating' as such without clearly stating what one is attempting to persuade people to do. The salesman is not just 'motivating' but aims to persuade his prospective customers to make the purchase. Management is not just 'motivating' but is aiming to persuade its employees to increase output and/or to reduce costs so as to improve profitability.

We see that 'motivation' is closely concerned with the centre of controversy, with the sharing out of income and wealth between those who work and those who employ. There is at present considerable danger of the whole subject coming into disrepute as some employers attempt to use it to persuade employees to increase profits without corresponding gains for the employees themselves.

But there are other ways of looking at the will to work, namely from the point of view of the individual and from that of the community. Consider the point of view of the individual. Some time ago I wrote about some of the incentives necessary to motivate professional employees to higher productivity {6}. I then said that frustration arises from the work they are asked to do, from the way in which it is organised, from the lack of incentive to do well. What was needed was to utilise the potential of those who are not working at full capacity and ability, and to provide corresponding incentive payments for professional experience and excellence, in other words for knowledge, skill and experience.

So what we are looking at is the reaction of those who are employed to the impact of the style of management at work, that is to the way in which they are being treated at work, to the responsibility which they carry, to the extent to which work is imposed on them, to the extent and way in which they are rewarded for the work they do.

Payment by Results, Productivity Bargaining and Profit Sharing

Employees are paid with money and can be seen to be working for money. Hence pay can be related to output, the so called payment- by- results system. Management provides incentives, management rewards effort.

In any kind of payment-by-results system, the fundamental considerations are how the workers' pay depends on the output achieved and on the extent to which he shares in the increased value he produces.

It seems that in the Unites States roughly 10% of employees respond to incentive schemes. The other 90% hold back, restricting output in response to the style of management, perhaps because increased rate of output with resulting increased earnings in the past soon resulted in the rates being cut back so that workers had to work at the higher rate but gained less, or because inflation eroded the value of their earnings.

However, there is little point in paying according to increased production when the rate of production is determined by the speed of the assembly belt or by the process, since these are not under the direct control of the worker. This is happening more frequently in highly industrialised societies, say when considering automated production lines or when introducing roboticised computer-controlled processes.

Where payment by results cannot be applied because the process is already highly controlled or operating at fixed speed then productivity bargaining is used which aims to introduce economies by different methods of working, sharing the gains with the work force in some negotiated proportion.

Increasing productivity means more than increasing output, means that capital equipment and men are more fully utilised, that goods are being produced more cheaply because overheads are lower in addition to the lower capital cost per unit produced.

But the argument again is about the extent to which the additional profits are shared between management and employees.

However, the reward of company directors {2}

> 'should relate to work done and to responsibility carried. Remuneration should depend on results, based on profit, through profit-sharing. The aim should be to motivate towards better performance.' and

> 'Directors consider they could share in the capital growth of the company, through share ownership and by way of share purchase and option schemes. Share ownership is regarded as assisting direct involvement while providing incentive through dividends and capital gain.'

The result aimed at is profit and the incentive is a share of the results obtained. Those who run organisations themselves would like to have a share in the enterprise, feel that common ownership assists involvement.

Job Satisfaction

Sisk {3} looks in some detail at whether there is a relationship between 'job satisfaction' and productivity. Herzberg considers that 'feelings of self-improvement, achievement, and the desire for the acceptance of greater responsibility' are more important than money for persuading people to increase productivity. He interviewed American engineers and accountants and on the whole they appear to have been quite frustrated. Sisk says that 'job satisfaction is but one of several factors making up the complex of needs ... and, as yet, there is no demonstrable relationship between job satisfaction and productivity'.

This means that there are other additional factors which need to be considered.

Remuneration, Job Satisfaction and Motivation

An investigation into the motivation of company directors {1} isolated motivating factors from those which were dissatisfying.

Figure 1 is reproduced from the report and illustrates the findings. It shows how strongly directors feel about each factor and just how important it is relative to other factors.

These factors were felt to provide reward and incentive, that is were worth straining to achieve. The degree to which they were lacking was at times felt to be dissatisfying.

All the factors are money factors, consist of material rewards <1>. Directors first and foremost work for remuneration and want a greater share of the benefits of ownership.

Interesting is that the question of job satisfaction just did not arise to any significant extent. On the whole the directors were satisfied with the work they were doing. Generally in position of considerable responsibility, they are aware that success or failure of the enterprise they direct depends on the decisions they make and that others are aware of this. Hence they may well be working for the greater power and luxury which wealth brings.

Herzberg considered job satisfaction was motivating but that money is not. But we have just seen that at least as far as directors are concerned, money is motivating and job satisfaction is not.

Directors have all the job satisfaction they need or want. They carry considerable responsibility and success often depends on individual effort. They have nicely and often luxuriously furnished offices, dine in the directors' dining room, have the benefit of a company car and last but not least work with pleasant colleagues in a pleasant way. It is because they have all the job satisfaction they want that money is important to them.

Figure 1
Motivation of Directors:
Type, Extent and Intensity of Motivating Factors

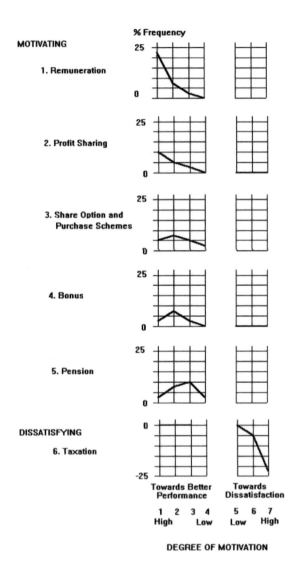

The American accountants and engineers investigated by Herzberg were, like other American professional employees and managers, considerably frustrated with the style of management and hence the importance of self-improvement, achievement, and the desire for greater responsibility as motivating factors. Money is of secondary importance to those who are frustrated but the need for job satisfaction is felt according to the degree of their frustration.

One wants that which one does not have, one works to achieve that which one needs and this could be either job satisfaction or money. The devout minister may leave his congregation and work in industry or teach because his pay as a minister is too low, the nurse will go on strike for the same reason. In both cases we see that job satisfaction in itself is not enough if one is paid too little. The teacher will go on strike for extra pay although teaching also can be very satisfying work. On the other hand the engineer may be so frustrated with the work he is doing, with the way the company's work is organised and with the way people work together at his place of work, that he will find another job even if this means a drop in income.

If one assumes that the worker is only working for the money he earns, then payment by results on its own would seem logical. But if money is important only up to the point where basic needs are satisfied then job satisfaction becomes more important. Both job satisfaction and money are needs dependent on which one of these one is deprived of or is looking for.

Hence the following definition {1} of 'motivation', of what people will work to achieve:

'Motivation towards better performance depends on the satisfaction of needs for responsibility, achievement, recognition and growth.

Needs are felt, and their intensity varies from one person to another and from time to time, and so does the extent to which they are motivating.

Behaviour is learned, earned reward encourages even better performance, thus reinforcing desired behaviour.'

It is what one does not have that one wants, one works to achieve that which one needs. Hence if we know what people need and want then we know what they will work for, and like working for, and so work well to achieve.

Attaining goals leads to feelings of self-respect, strength and confidence.

Few people are able to continue a pattern of achievement and success without the added encouragement provided by others recognising their achievements.

Continued failure and frustration and defeat can result in feelings of inadequacy and a withdrawal from competitive situations.

Persistent lack of rewards leads to a view of society as being hostile and unrewarding.

It is what one does not have that one wants, one works to achieve that which one needs.

Hence we can now look at the

Needs and Wants People Strive to Achieve

We have seen {8} that the professional employee's pay increases with age. It does so {4} because he absorbs and applies experience, because he then has the opportunity to use his enlarged knowledge and experience by working at a higher level, being paid more correspondingly. The rate at which his pay increases depends not only on his ability but also on the work and positions open to him, on the scope and opportunity provided by his employer or by the work he can find.

Hence what the individual wants and expects from the job, from the management, is to be given challenging work, to be backed by management and colleagues in carrying it out, and then to be rewarded by being given the chance to utilise the experience gained by being given the opportunity to work at a higher level with correspondingly higher pay.

The individual will generally progress according to a specific remuneration 'grade line' of his own <2>. Remuneration grade lines give the norm for individuals of a particular trade or profession at their own level of ability and success. When an individual's level of working and income drop below his line then he is falling behind colleagues of his own age doing similar work elsewhere and feels this and becomes frustrated. Frustration on the part of an individual, and his finally leaving the work unit, are both detrimental to the performance of the work unit {4}.

Progress according to these remuneration grade lines is the norm, is the way in which others doing similar work at the same age are in fact progressing.

The individual becomes aware of and assesses any changes away from his remuneration grade line. Moving up and moving down are felt to be promotion and demotion, respectively, relative to colleagues of same age working in the same profession at the same level. Those progressing according to their remuneration grade line are fulfilling their expectation, those improving their position feel that they are doing well, both generally feel satisfied with their own progress relative to their colleagues.

People are aware of their own position in the community, of the pecking order and of their place in it <3>. Changes are noticed and felt. Indeed people are often intensely concerned about the threat of increasing differentials and about whether they are moving up or down, gaining or losing.

In other words, people strive to maintain their position, in this way striving to receive their share of the increasing national income and wealth.

In addition people are both aware of and concerned about the large differences in the standard of living which exist between different countries. Their commitment to their own community depends on the style of management and on the success of the community, depends on the extent to which the community serves them and satisfies their needs. In other words, people will strive for the community to the extent to which they see it as satisfying their needs or as a means for satisfying their needs.

Hence we can now look at the range of needs and wants people strive to achieve.

First there are certain basic needs which have to be satisfied if people are to exist and survive, such as:

> Shelter and food, clothing and warmth.
>
> Affection and esteem.
>
> Friendly and trustful co-operation and companionship.
>
> Security from external threats (i.e. protection from attack).

Then other needs make themselves felt, such as:

> Independence from domination by others (e.g. because of need).
>
> Security from internal threats.
>
> Housing, education, good health.
>
> Help when in need.
>
> Constructive leisure activities.

To which we can add the ones we have just discussed, namely:

> Challenging work, which means scope to work at increasing levels of skill and usefulness and thus of pay, to the maximum of one's ability.

Maintaining, and the chance for improving, one's position relative to colleagues.

Recognition of success by others (leads to feeling of self-respect, strength and confidence).

Fair share of the national income and wealth.

Fair share of the international income and wealth.

These then are the needs and wants people strive to achieve, indeed struggle to achieve. People will co-operate with each other, will work hard and well to satisfy these needs and gain much satisfaction from doing so.

The Struggle for Independence and a Good Life

Now if you look again at the list of needs and wants then the one thing which stands out is that they are not special. This is what people need and want, this is what people are striving to achieve and nowadays this what people could have. And yet all around we see people struggling at the different stages to achieve the next step.

That progress arises only as the result of struggle is expressed in many different ways. Consider it from the point of view of the workplace. No matter how paternal the company, the employees know that whatever they are getting arises from the self-interest of the employer and is likely to be the result of confrontation and of a balance between negotiating strengths. And yet commitment to the objectives of the owners and directors, for example a company's objectives, comes from the extent to which the company serves its employees, comes from the extent to which it helps them to achieve their needs and wants.

We saw again and again, in the reports on the style of management and on work and pay, that there is no real conflict of interest between those who lead and those who work. What we saw was that what is good for the employees is good for the owners, that what is good for the people is good for the leadership, that what benefits the people also benefits the leadership.

When co-operation pays so handsomely, how come that we see so much confrontation and struggle, how come that all around us we see progress being achieved only as the result of struggle.

What stands out is that the confrontation is not between employers and employees, between management and labour, between state and citizens since there are companies, enterprises and administrations which have the backing and co-operation of those who work with and for them. The confrontation and struggle appear to be against those who wish to run enterprises and wish to organise society on authoritarian lines <11>, appears to be a struggle against authoritarian minds.

There is a point of balance within each organisation or administration and in the democracies this ranges from 'authoritarian' to the fully participative common ownership enterprise. However, to understand the causes of the confrontation and struggle, let us look at the confrontation between fully authoritarian owners or rulers and their employees or people, let us look at what people do to achieve their needs and wants by seeing what it is that people struggle for.

Figure 2 illustrates the basic confrontation. There is nothing here which has not been mentioned or discussed either here or elsewhere in these seven reports on community leadership and management. Authoritarian owners and rulers (no matter whether 'left' or 'right') wish to dominate and control employees and people for the sake of personal income, wealth and power. Employees and people counter this by behaving in ways which encourage trustful co-operation and co-operate with each other.

Figure 2

Basic Confrontation

THE AUTHORITARIAN MIND	PEOPLE (AS INDIVIDUALS)	COMMUNITY
Owners, directors (and establishment). Rulers, state (and party hierarchy).	Employees, Citizens.	All the people together.
Authoritarian.	Need independence from domination by others (e.g. from being oppressed and exploited because of need).	Co-operate with each other (participative organisation)
Want greater income, wealth, power, i.e.	Want to develop and apply own abilities and skills	Want to achieve their individual

increased profits and control and domination over others.

to the full.

aims (i.e. for the common good).

Require work to be done at the lowest rate of pay. <4>

Require scope to work at increasing levels of skill and usefulness and corresponding increasing acknowledgement.

Jointly wish to achieve the highest possible standard of living and quality of life;

locally, country-wide, world-wide.

I.e. aim to reduce the cost of work (labour costs) by:

1. Pressure of real or imposed needs (e.g. unemployment). <7>

1. Co-operate with each other to provide help when in need.

2. Condoning and encouraging behaviour which weakens the individual and the community, which sets people against each other. <6>

2. Behave in ways which encourage trustful co-operation and companionship.

3. Lowering the standard of living of the community as a whole compared with other communities (e.g. between countries). <5>

The 'community' includes all and in this context people organise their affairs and administration on participative lines to safeguard their independence and to achieve their individual and common aims.

It is this which underlies democracy and authoritarian minds (examples being owners as well as rulers) confront and struggle with communal institutions so as to take them over and make them serve themselves instead of the people, instead of serving the policy-making body.

This means that the two sides confront each other not just at the place of work but in all communal institutions. It is because of this that people's needs and wants are achieved only as the result of struggle.

People Work Willingly for What They Need and Want

In the previous two sections we saw just what people need and want and strive to achieve and that their needs are only satisfied and that their wants are only achieved as the result of struggle, as the result of struggle for independence and a good life.

We also saw that the struggle takes place in all aspects of life and while the confrontation in, and the struggle for control of, communal institutions is discussed in more detail in appendix 1, we can now fit the parts together to form the complete picture.

The whole struggle is described and illustrated by figure 3 'Peoples' Needs and Wants, Achievements and Objectives: The Struggle for Independence and Good Life'. It lists the aims and methods of the authoritarian mind, of those who wish to oppress so as to exploit. It also lists what individuals are striving to achieve, that is their needs and wants. What we have seen is that people have to struggle all the way and the illustration also shows what has already been achieved in democratic countries and what remains to be achieved.

What I have described here is a list of needs and wants and thus policy aims, the successive achievement of which gives a sequence and a measure of noted and felt progress which should give a feeling of forward movement, growth and satisfaction.

However, one's resources are generally limited and one needs to decide how to allocate funds between main areas such as (a) economic growth, (b) national security, (c) an internal rising standard of living combined with (d) a liberalisation from authority, towards greater freedom both in government and in the work place, combined with (e) ever greater participation in policy setting in government as well as in the work place.

The knowledge, methods, techniques and measures described in this set of reports enable one to obtain a favourable balance between the requirements of those who lead and those who work.

Independence for some may mean self-employment with guaranteed independence but for others may mean the right to work (employment) and pay.

People strive for satisfying work, for social security and for independence, want to be masters of their own destiny through self-employment. They would like the community to back the individual in this, the individual in turn contributing to the community so that it can help others and protect all.

One needs to be concerned about the value placed on different kinds of work, for example about the extent to which those who are well paid serve the rulers or owners instead of the community, about internal differentials and about the extent to which the style of management at the place of work and countrywide is authoritarian, not forgetting that in an emergency an authoritarian organisation can work well but that precautions need to be taken at all times against the authoritarian mind taking over participative institutions and organisations.

One has to go beyond this and consider not only one's own position within one's own community but that of one's own community within the world at large, consider the extent to which some countries are exploiting others. We are not just concerned about an unequal division of land, of the means of production (i.e. capital) but need to include profiteering from raw materials. And this means that there have to be certain limits beyond which differentials may not be allowed to increase. This applies equally well between countries as it does within a country between different levels or occupations.

There are at present some important and crucial areas in which the community is under attack from within and where the community needs to defend itself to ensure its safety and to regain its strength. Some of these are discussed in the report which deals with the question of social responsibility.

Figure 3

People's Needs and Wants, Achievements and Objectives: The Struggle for Independence and Good Life

BASIC CONFRONTATION		STRUGGLE FOR INDEPENDENCE AND GOOD LIFE	
1	**2**	**3**	**4**
The Authoritarian Mind. Its Aims and Methods <9>	What People (As Individuals) Are Striving to Achieve <13>, (i.e. their Needs and Wants)	What has been Achieved by the Community in at least some Communities	What Remains to be Achieved
Owners, directors (and establishment)	People as employees	Community: All the people co-operating with each other to achieve their aims.	
Rulers, state (and party hierarchy)	People as citizens		

1	**2**	**3**	**4**
Want greater income, wealth and power, i.e. want increased profits, want control and domination over others (oppress so	Existence: Shelter and food, clothing and warmth

Affection and esteem | Family unity and strength

Social security benefits (corresponding to a minimum wage) to maintain specified level of existence | Secure and strong family |

1	2	3	4
as to exploit)	Friendly and trustful co-operation and companionship	Freedom of speech and of propagation of ideas and opinions	Generally socially responsible behaviour such as that laid down in the Ten Commandments
	Security from external threats (protection from attack)	Strong armed forces and associated services to prevent attack by possible competitors or attackers	Effective international co-operation (to prevent aggression against the people)
	Independence from domination by others (e.g. because of need)	The people provide the money which their government, authorised by and acting for the people, requires to spend for the community. It is given through direct and indirect taxation according to ability to pay	Participative organisation and leadership instead of overlordship. Participation in decision making Power sharing Common ownership (i.e. secure independence)

1	**2**	**3**	**4**

Aim to reduce the cost of work (labour) by

1. Condoning and encouraging behaviour	Security from internal threats	Legislation and enforcement preventing people and	Control of power by the community in civil and

which
weakens the
individual
and the
community,
which sets
people
against each
other.

enterprises
from behaving
in ways which
would harm
themselves or
others

military fields.
I.e. to ensure
that such
power serves
only the
community,
i.e. is used
responsibly

More effective
ways of
preventing the
authoritarian
mind from
infiltrating and
taking over the
community's
institutions,
administration
and
organisations.

Educating the
people in the
reality of life
and
community-
orientated
leadership
training (see
this set of
seven reports)

Effective
accountability
of the
leadership to
the
community.

2. Pressure of real or imposed needs.	Housing, education, good health	Subsidised rented housing and subsidised home ownership. Free education, grants to cover educational fees and living expenses while studying.
		Good medical (country-wide) national community health service available to all free of charge.
	Help when in need	Unemployment benefit.
		Redundancy compensation.
		Retirement pension, fully transferable and inflation-proofed pension rights.
		Health insurance, i.e. benefit payments to those unable to earn a living because of illness.

Constructive leisure activities   Interest development training (free or at a nominal charge)

1	2	3	4
Require work to be done at the lowest possible rate.	Challenging work, i.e. scope to work at increasing levels of skill and usefulness and thus of pay, to the maximum of one's ability. <12>	Merit increases, defined by 'national remuneration scales' given as a matter of course <8>	
	Maintaining, and scope for improving, one's position relative to colleagues. <12>		People should have scope for working at the highest level of responsibility which can be carried by them during any particular period <8>.
	Recognition by others of one's success (leads to feelings of self-respect, strength and confidence).		

1	2	3	4
Reward those who serve the authoritarian mind to gain and keep what it wants (see what is listed in this column)	Fair share of the national income, assets and wealth	Automatic cost of living increases which compensate fully <8>. Separate betterment increases which provide direct participation in country's prosperity <8>. Share in increasing national wealth through shorter working week and longer holidays <8>.	The pattern of differentials is clearly shown by the 'National Remuneration Pattern' <10>. We need to develop appropriate income and wealth differentials {5} according to service to the community. Hence one needs to have clear ideas about what one is paying for, i.e. about the community's needs and wants, and have corresponding measures of progress and success. The income of those at the top could be not more than two times the minimum income <14, 15>

Aim at lowering the standard of living of the community as a whole compared with other communities (e.g. between countries to reduce their own labour costs so as to increase profits).	Fair share of the international income, assets and wealth	Community's progress makes itself felt in real terms such as by an increase in the standard of living, by a better, more secure and richer life	The differential between best and worst countries should be not more than two, using appropriate measures of inequality such as income and wealth per head of population and measures of health, education, housing quality and material consumption, i.e. measures of physical, mental and material well-being, of security, freedom and happiness. <15>
Aim at increasing their power by taking over other units, organisations, countries. Use means such as loans, conditional aid, professional expertise and manpower to tie and later control the recipient.		Aid and support between democratic countries	Some way of bringing those who have fallen behind up to the level of the best but also ways of ensuring two-way traffic, of mutual support, of support of democratic principles and practice.

1	2	3	4
People cease to care, work only for the money, tend to produce shoddy and unreliable goods.			Identification with and commitment to the community results from the knowledge that the individual serves the community which in turn serves the individual, that what benefits the one also benefits the other.

Notes and References

Notes

< 1>   Taxation is a matter of social policy and unrelated to one's performance in the work place. Paying much tax may be dissatisfying but extra money resulting from reduced taxation is unrelated to one's performance and because of this is not motivating.

< 2>   See {8}, 'Individual Incomes'.

< 3>   See {8}, figure 3 'National Remuneration Pattern' and Figure 2 'Remuneration Increments ('Betterment')'.

< 4>   See {8}, 'The Cost of Getting Work Done'.

< 5>   Discussed in {9}, 'Making Ends Meet'.

< 6>   See {7}, 'Appendix 1'.

< 7>   See {7}, 'Authoritarian Organisation'.

<8>   See {4} and {6}.

< 9>   From figure 2 'Basic Confrontation'.

<10> See {8}, figure 3 and text.

<11> See {7}, 'Authoritarian Organisation' and 'Appendix 1'.

<12> See {8} about 'National Remuneration Scales' (figure 1 and text) and about 'Salary administration and manpower planning'.

<13> From chapter 'Needs and Wants People Strive to Achieve'.

<14> See p.18, column 3, 'Automatic cost of living increases ...' .

<15> See {8}, 'The Way Ahead'.

<16> See chapter 'The Struggle for Independence and a Good Life'.

References

{1} Work, Remuneration and Motivation of Directors,
Manfred Davidmann,
Social Organisation Ltd

{2} The Effective Board: A Study of the Work and Remuneration of Directors,
Manfred Davidmann,
Social Organisation Ltd

{3} Principles of Management,
H.L. Sisk,
Edward Arnold

{4} Salary Administration and Manpower Planning,
Manfred Davidmann,
Social Organisation Ltd

{5} Appropriate Pay,
Manfred Davidmann,
Social Organisation Ltd

{6} Professional Engineers' Career Prospects,
Manfred Davidmann,
Chemical and Process Engineering

{7} In 'Management and Leadership:
Local, National, Multinational (Global),
Principles and Practice'
Manfred Davidmann
ISBN 978-0-85192-057-3
See chapter 2: 'Style of Management and Leadership'

{8} Work and Pay, Incomes and Differentials:
Employer, Employee and Community
Manfred Davidmann, 1981-1995, 2007
solhaam.org

{9} In 'Management and Leadership:
Local, National, Multinational (Global),
Principles and Practice'
Manfred Davidmann
ISBN 978-0-85192-057-3
See chapter 9: 'Inflation, Balance of Payments and
Currency Exchange Rates'
which also discusses how base (general) interest
rates affect share prices and pensions, and the
struggle for a bigger share.

Appendix 1

The Struggle for Independence, Against the Authoritarian Mind, which is Taking Place in Boardrooms, Government, Trade Unions and Other Institutions

What is good for the people is good for the leadership, what benefits the people also benefits the leadership. And yet although co-operation pays so handsomely we see all around us that progress is achieved only as the result of confrontation and struggle against those who wish to run enterprises and organise society on authoritarian lines, that progress is achieved only as the result of struggle against authoritarian minds. The two sides confront each other not just at the place of work but in all communal institutions. <16>

Here we are not directly concerned with this part of the confrontation but an example from the boardrooms of our companies will illustrate its relevance.

Take a board of directors consisting of chairman, managing director, three executive directors and two part-time directors. The board exists to serve the interests of the shareholders who own the enterprise and there are no worker directors. The managing director and the three executive directors are full-time employees of the company and the three executive directors are departmental heads. The managing director is responsible to the Board for the day-to-day running of the company and the three departmental heads are responsible to him for the work of their departments.

The board of directors can be represented by this chart:

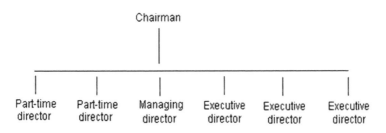

In practice, the organisation chart is more likely to look like:

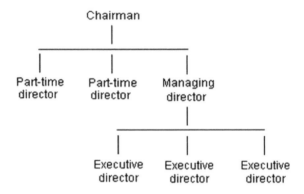

The managing director is unlikely to admit that shortcomings could be due to those he controls or due to inadequate organisation or management. The three departmental heads who are also directors and who are responsible to him for their work as departmental heads are unlikely to argue with or contradict their superior at board meetings.

The chairman generally represents the shareholders and so do the part-time directors. The part-time directors owe allegiance only to the shareholders and may freely criticise the way in which the company is managed.

It can be seen that the three directors who represent the owners may be outvoted by the other four directors whose first allegiance is to the company's executive, to the managing director.

The Board's policy-making is supposed to safeguard the interests of the shareholders and thus chairman and part-time directors can speak up on any issue. But in this case policy-making is unduly influenced by the managing director who may now influence policy as he sees fit. If he wishes to organise matters so as to give himself more and perhaps even full control and authority for the sake of personal power, then it is unlikely that this board would argue that participative management is more difficult but also more profitable.

The same confrontation between on the one hand elected representative policy-making bodies, and on the other hand those who are supposed to put their policies into effect, can be seen in many areas. For example there are the arguments about the executive powers of the President of the United States, between President and USA's representative legislative assemblies (Congress and Senate). A further example is that of the trade union General Secretary who shortly after election attempts to change the rules so as to make his appointment more secure or permanent.

Another example is that the Histadrut, Israel's general federation of trade unions, decided about twenty years ago that worker participation in decision making was to be introduced in the Histadrut's own enterprises. Twenty years later the indications are that workers in Histadrut owned enterprises still have a long way to go before achieving this.

Even when the annual conference of a political party consists of local delegates elected by secret ballot from among all the local membership we are likely to see friction if not confrontation between the party's executive and the policy setting annual conference. In Israel the otherwise very democratic system of proportional representation which gives minorities a voice and power according to their numerical strength, has been defeated by the way in which prospective members of the Knesset (government) are selected by party hierarchies.

What is characteristic of a community is that it consists of all the people together co-operating with each other for the common good and their joint struggle against authoritarian minds which wish to oppress people so as to exploit them.

Individuals and the community are struggling for independence and a good life, are struggling to establish co-operative institutions and enterprises, are struggling internally against the authoritarian mind taking over their leaders and thus their co-operative enterprises.

This is a constant struggle. So how come that the authoritarian mind is so persistent and how come that it can persuade people to behave in ways which are against the interests of the people? How come that the people have in the past been made to behave, and are even now at times behaving, in ways which serve the authoritarian mind at enormous cost to the people as a whole?

The underlying causes, the way in which people are persuaded into serving the authoritarian mind, the way in which institutions have been infiltrated and taken over, the way the leadership of the people has in the past been turned against the people, the way in which public opinion is manipulated and the means used for doing this, need to be explored and exposed.

It is a struggle for men's minds and then for their bodies, on the one hand towards love of servitude and at best mere existence but on the other hand towards love of independence and towards freedom and a good life.

Chapter 17

Quotable Quotes about Democracy in the Real World

The Meaning of Democracy

(Contains) a detailed step-by-step listing of what people are struggling to achieve, their needs and wants, their achievements and objectives. This progression shows underdeveloped and developed people as they are, human beings at different stages of an identical struggle for a better life against those who wish to profit from their condition.

And you can assess how far the country/community you are living in has advanced in this struggle for independence and a good life for all, or where you are yourself on this scale.

> From
> Chapter 16:
> 'The Will to Work: What People Struggle to Achieve'
> Manfred Davidmann, 1981, 1989, 1995
>
> Highlights are Figure 1 (Motivation of Directors) and Figure 3 (People's Needs and Wants, Achievements and Objectives: The Struggle for Independence and a Good Life).

Participative (democratic) organisation rests on the population electing representatives, on the basis of each person having one vote. Representatives are responsible to, and accountable to, the population for putting into effect policies decided by the population.

What underlies participative organisation (democracy) is decision-taking by the people at the level of the people.

Policies state what has to be done and by when it has to be done. What needs to be stressed is that in a participative (democratic) organisation policies are decided by a well-informed population at the level of the population and that these policies then become binding on management or government.

And representatives, governments or government officials do not have the authority or right to reduce or sign away the participative (democratic) rights of the electors, of the population.

In an authoritarian organisation the policy decisions are taken at the top or near the top by the hierarchy (establishment) and are binding on the organisation's members. ... Authoritarian organisation is the opposite of democracy and underlies dictatorship.

What we see all around us is conflict between authoritarian minds wishing to dominate, control and exploit on the one hand and, on the other hand, citizens wishing to maintain and improve the standard of living and quality of life for the population as a whole by democratic (grassroots level) decision-taking.

What we see is top-level leaderships trying to take over decision-taking from the population.

We can see the struggle in all organisations and at all levels. It is a struggle against authoritarian management or government for the right to take decisions. And in all democratic organisations it is a struggle against the authoritarian mind taking over the decision-taking.

So the real struggle is not between political left and right, but is a struggle for participation (the right to take decisions).

> From
> Chapter 11:
> 'Democracy Under Attack: Top-level Leadership
> and Decision-making'
> Manfred Davidmann

> And
> Chapter 6:
> 'Multinational Summits and Agreements,
> Top-level Decision-making and Democracy'
> Manfred Davidmann

In the working environment we see a world-wide struggle to achieve a humane way of life, each family, person or community struggling to advance at their own level of development, struggling against those who wish to dominate, exploit, oppress. A struggle whose successful outcome depends on trustful co-operation, companionship and teamwork.

We know that dominating does not work in normal circumstances. Authoritarian organisations are much less effective than participative ones. In authoritarian organisations morale is low, people cease to care and tend to work against each other instead of co-operating with each other for the benefit of the organisation. Which applies equally well to a family.

> From
> 'God and People:
> The Social Laws and Social System Underlying
> Judaism, Christianity, Islam and Democracy'
> Manfred Davidmann
> ISBN 978-0-85192-054-2
> see chapter 5: 'Family, Community, Sex and the Individual'

Participative organisation and co-operation result in economic success. More participative countries have a higher standard of living than those with more authoritarian forms of government. Higher by about three times.

A move towards greater centralisation, towards more authoritarian government, corresponds to a more restricted life and lower standard of living. A move towards greater participation corresponds to a higher quality of life and a higher standard of living.

Take the USA. A democratic country with high standard of living, a country of great contrasts. Great poverty and suffering, great riches. Much oppression but there is no doubt about the way the population is enabled to struggle and is struggling to achieve a better life for themselves and their children, about their appreciation of the value of democracy (participation) and its principles. A people who have been, and are, achieving much.

> From
> 'Management and Leadership:
> Local, National, Multinational (Global),
> Principles and Practice'
> Manfred Davidmann
> ISBN 978-0-85192-057-3
> See chapter 2: 'Style of Management and Leadership'

When talking about pay, incomes and differentials, then we are dealing with matters which are at the centre of confrontation and conflict and around which rage controversy and strife. We are dealing with matters which determine how one man stands in relation to another, with something which depends on negotiation and bargaining between those who employ and those who are employed. The result is that almost all one sees about pay and differentials is biased towards one side or the other and both points of view are then equally misleading.

> From
> 'Management and Leadership:
> Local, National, Multinational (Global),
> Principles and Practice'
> Manfred Davidmann
> ISBN 978-0-85192-057-3
> See chapter 8: 'Work and Pay'

The National Remuneration Pattern is factual and reliable. It shows the relative value placed on different kinds of work in the United Kingdom. It is largely determined by employers.

The pattern tends to be applied through national or industry-wide centralised negotiations. The employer sets a rate for the job which is not what he can afford to pay but is simply the least he has to pay to get the work done.

At the top are the owners or those who work directly for them, at the bottom is the mass of wage earners. It is a pattern of differentials which rewards service to the owners and their establishment rather than ability or service to the community. And so the nurse, the minister, the fireman, the policeman and the teacher are at present paid comparatively little for the work they do.

Those who provide jobs and money have power over those who need to work so as to live. This applies also to those who have the power to give or not to give in national and local government, and the civil service. Putting the interests of the owners and of their representatives before that of the community is probably the main cause of our deteriorating environment and of lowering the quality of life.

> From
> 'Management and Leadership:
> Local, National, Multinational (Global),
> Principles and Practice'
> Manfred Davidmann
> ISBN 978-0-85192-057-3
> See chapter 8: 'Work and Pay'

The Right to Education

People are entitled to free education to the highest level they can reach, dependent only on their skills and abilities.

A key problem of communist state education appears to have been that people were fed much ideological abstract nice-sounding waffle. This, and the consequent inability of people to think clearly and work through their problems, appears to have been a major cause of the suffering of the Russian people after the collapse of the state-communist social system. And of authoritarians taking over Yugoslavia's advanced social system by setting people against each other and breaking up the country.

> From
> 'Management and Leadership:
> Local, National, Multinational (Global),
> Principles and Practice'
> Manfred Davidmann
> ISBN 978-0-85192-057-3
> See chapter 2: 'Style of Management and Leadership'

People need to learn to reject abstract waffle as being imprecise, meaningless and misleading.

It is not good enough for students to be asked to provide textbook answers to textbook questions. People need to be taught to think, reason, evaluate, assess the relevance and reliability of information.

> From
> Chapter 15:
> 'Using Words to Communicate Effectively'
> Manfred Davidmann

The Right to Decide

In 'The Meaning of Democracy' we saw that

> In an authoritarian organisation the policy decisions are taken at the top or near the top by the hierarchy (establishment) and are binding on the organisation's members. We see secretive top-level decision-taking. Authoritarian organisation is the opposite of democracy and underlies dictatorship.
>
> What underlies participative organisation (democracy) is decision-taking by the people at the level of the people.
>
> So what needs to be stressed is that in a participative (democratic) organisation policies are decided by a well-informed population at the level of the population and that policies then become binding on management or government.
>
> So the real struggle is not between political left and right, but is a struggle for participation (the right to take decisions).

> From
> Chapter 11:
> Democracy Under Attack:
> Top-level Leadership and Decision-making'
> Manfred Davidmann (1998)

Decisions about work should be taken by those doing the work or close to the work being done.

We decide what we do or what we do not do. It is individuals who take decisions, who are responsible for taking them and thus accountable for the consequences of the decisions they take or fail to take.

> From
> 'Cooperatives and Cooperation:
> Causes of Failure, Guidelines for Success'
> Manfred Davidmann
> ISBN 978-0-85192-056-6

See this also for a comprehensive discussion of the electing, appointing and appraisal of managers, directors and elected representatives, of the right to ownership, the right to know, the right to be heard, and of work, pay and differentials.

The Right to Strike

The slave has to work whether he likes it or not. Slavery denies to the enslaved their basic human rights. The slave is treated by the master like an unfeeling production unit, is kept and maintained while productive.

The master in effect owns and controls the slave through what he can force the slave to do by means of the laws of the land and by force of economic necessity.

The free man may withdraw his labour. He enters into a voluntary agreement with someone else in which he agrees to carry out some specified work in return for a specified amount of pay. If there is disagreement between them he may freely withdraw his labour. This is a most essential right, the right of every citizen, of every worker, to associate with others and withdraw his labour, to go on strike.

People are enslaved when they are forced to work through need, have to work to survive. They are enslaved to the extent to which they are forced to accept mere survival existence in return for the work they do. They are free to the extent to which they are able to choose freely between one employer and another, to the extent to which they are backed by a comprehensive system of social security and services if falling on difficult times.

A workforce which cannot withdraw its labour at will is either oppressed or enslaved. A free people have the right to strike and can exercise this right, supporting those who exercise it.

From
The Right to Strike
Manfred Davidmann, 1996
solhaam.org

Role of Experts

Experts inform and advise about what should, can or cannot be done and about likely consequences either way.

Experts must be independent, must not derive income, benefit or advantages from companies or interested sources, or from vested interests, or have vested interests, which could bias their advice one way or the other.

The role of experts is to advise.

From
Chapter 14:
'Corrupted Economics and Misguided (Misleading) Experts'
Manfred Davidmann (1998)

Selecting and Electing Representatives

Proportional Representation: 'Closed-list' and 'Open-list' Systems

Voting by proportional representation (PR) decides how many candidates of a party are elected. If 300 seats are available and the party gets one-third of the votes, then it gets one-third of the seats, that is it gets 100 seats.

If the party put forward a list of 300 candidates, only 100 can become representatives.

With a "closed list" system of PR, the electors vote for the party and not for a local candidate. They thus vote for the party's list. In the above example, it is the first-named 100 names on the list which become representatives.

With an "open list" system the electors have the chance of voting for candidates of their choice from the party's list.

From
Chapter 11:
'Democracy Under Attack:
Top-level Leadership and Decision-making'
Manfred Davidmann (1998)

Closed-list System

Whether or not one is placed on the list, and one's position on the list, determines whether one is elected or not.

With this system it is not really the electorate which decides whether one is elected as a local representative. Whether one is elected depends on whether one is placed on the list and on one's top-to-bottom position on the list. So whether one is elected depends on the party leader or leadership.

So one's chance of being elected depends on doing as told by leader or leadership, on supporting their policies, instead of depending on serving one's constituents (local electors), instead of being responsible and accountable to the electors, to the community one is supposed to represent and act for.

The higher up one's name appears on the list, the more likely is one to be elected, the more likely is it that one benefits from the high salary, excellent allowances, good working conditions and good pension rights which go with the job. Loyalty to leader or leadership replaces loyalty to electors.

It is the grassroots membership which should select and decide who is to represent them. The party leadership seems to be close to taking over both functions.

What we see taking place with a closed-list system is far removed from being responsible and accountable to one's local electors, to the local community, for the way in which one represents them and looks after their interests both at local and national level. Democratic decision-taking is reversed by a system of closed-list proportional representation as decision-taking by representatives is replaced with obedience to dictates from the top.

> From
> Chapter 11:
> 'Democracy Under Attack: Top-level Leadership
> and Decision-making'
> Manfred Davidmann (1998)

UK Members of European Parliament (MEPs)

There was widespread criticism from Labour MEPs, the Liberal Democrats and constitutional reform groups when the Labour government proposed to change the selecting and voting for UK MEPs to one which allowed parties rather than the electorate to select who was to be their MEP.

A position near the top of a party list would be crucial to success because seats would be allocated proportionately to the party, not the individual.

From
Chapter 10:
'What People are Struggling Against: How Society
is Organised for Controlling and Exploiting People'
Manfred Davidmann

Proportional Representation in Israel

In Israel the democratic system of proportional representation has been defeated by the way in which prospective members of the Knesset (government) are selected by party hierarchies and also by the way in which, after an election, minority parties can combine to replace the majority party. {3}

Reason would suggest that the largest parties (which must include the majority party) should (have to) get together and compromise (say by referendum on alternative policies, if they cannot agree otherwise). ....

From
Chapter 11:
'Democracy Under Attack:
Top-level Leadership and Decision-making'
Manfred Davidmann (1998)

Top-level Decision-taking and Democracy

Similarly, would it not be a good idea for each member of a government, each elected representative, to state in public what they personally are likely to gain, or lose, from the way they are voting on a particular legislation.

I feel that lists of such gains and losses may make interesting reading, for example about the recent changes by a conservative government to UKs local government taxation, from a 'Council Rate' (depending on property value) to a 'Poll Tax' (depending on number of resident people, on size of family) to a 'Council Tax' (Poll Tax amended because of public protest).

From
Chapter 14:
'Corrupted Economics and Misguided (Misleading) Experts'
Manfred Davidmann (1998)

Far-reaching decisions are to be taken affecting not just the many people working so selflessly and well throughout the NHS (National

Health Service) but the whole population, its health and thus our future. It thus seems surprising that the Inquiry report's far-reaching recommendations could be considered for implementation, and for speedy implementation at that, without a wide-ranging debate in Parliament and among the community at large on the basis of full information.

From
Reorganising the National Health Service:
An Evaluation of the Griffiths Report
Manfred Davidmann, (1984, 1985, 1995)
solhaam.org

Following the publication of Manfred Davidmann's evaluation with its request for a wide-ranging debate in Parliament, the government held a debate. The future of Britain's National Health Service was discussed in Parliament on a Friday afternoon in an 'Adjournment Debate', which means that no vote was taken. Only about 25 Members of Parliament were present.

In 1979 the UKs oil wells started to produce and the UK became a net exporter of oil, as far as I know the only one of the industrialised countries to be producing more oil than it consumed, extremely well off as a result. A conservative (Tory) government was elected in the same year, harvesting the benefits and staying in power for 18 years. But by 1997 poverty and wealth differentials had increased by so much, and the rights and social security of the working population had been reduced to such an extent, that it was clear that this time the Labour party would be elected.

Before the general election (May 1997) the Labour party's leadership changed and under the new leadership some fundamental changes were introduced.

The Annual Conference of the Labour party consisted of delegates from local branches and was policy setting. Resolutions, proposed policies, were submitted by local Labour party branches, debated by delegates at the conference. If passed then it was up to the party's executive (its leadership) to implement the policy, to put it into effect. The decisions were mandatory, had to be put into effect.

So the Labour party's annual conference took binding decisions on policy proposals brought up by grassroots membership. They decided policy which the executive had to follow and put into effect.

In the autumn of 1997 the conference voted for a system which transferred the choice of what could be debated from grassroots membership to a policy commission chaired by the party leader {16}.

This in effect took away a vital aspect of decision-taking from the working population and placed it in the hands of leader and leadership.

In January 1998 it was announced that forty-five policy forums were to be set up in which members would be invited to express their views on policies, from social issues to local government and that such views should eventually work through to the annual party conference.

Although members would be able to discuss policy, it seems the leadership can either take note or else ignore the proceedings. {17}

The annual conference ceased to decide policies, ceased to decide what had to be done. Instead of deciding mandatory policies based on direct policy proposals from local branches, the annual conference became a talking-shop, discussing and expressing views on subjects selected and approved by the leadership.

So a continuing process appears to be taking place which seems to be aimed at concentrating decision-taking in the hands of the top-level party leadership.

> From
> Chapter 11:
> 'Democracy Under Attack:
> Top-level Leadership and Decision-making'
> Manfred Davidmann (1998)

Manfred Davidmann laid down in 'Multinational Summits and Agreements, Top-level Decision-taking and Democracy', maxims such as

> Representatives, governments or government officials do not have the authority or right to override, reduce or sign away the participative (democratic) rights of the electors, of the population.

> No elected representative, government or government employee has an overriding right or the authority

> 1. to hand over to corporations (that is to those who own and control them), or to any other organisation or to anyone else, an overriding control over the present and future, economic and social, welfare of the people, or

> 2. to sign away democratic rights of their people for the self-determination of key fundamental aspects of their lives.

> Socially responsible and caring governmental legislation has to take precedence over the profit-motivated activities of corporations.

Decision-taking by leaderships has to be replaced by decision-taking at the level of the people.

The real struggle is not between political left and right, but is a struggle for participation (the right to take decisions).

From
Chapter 10:
'What People are Struggling Against:
How Society is Organised for Controlling and Exploiting People'
Manfred Davidmann (1999)

And
Chapter 6:
'Multinational Summits and Agreements,
Top-level Decision-making and Democracy'
Manfred Davidmann (2002)

and see:
Social Concept (Policies) of the Russian Orthodox Church:
Letter to the Russians
Manfred Davidmann, 2004
solhaam.org

So profits and power are apparently being maximised regardless of the cost to others, to the community. Without care or concern for the condition, standard of living or quality of life of the working population. Without being concerned about the enormous human suffering which results.

What we see are consequences of decisions made at the top, and the results of putting them into effect. Results and consequences which at times make the decisions seem so brutal that they appear inhuman.

What underlies democracy is decision-taking by the people at the level of the people. But what we see is top-level leaderships trying to take over decision-taking from the population.

Secretive top-level multinational meetings and agreements negate democratic government and decision-taking, without having overriding authority or right to do so.

But representatives, governments or government officials do not have the authority or right to override, reduce or sign away the participative (democratic) rights of the electors, of the population.

Multinational Summits and Agreements

And that a situation has been created in which the nature of profit-motivated and profit-orientated multinationals threatens human independence and freedom. {5}

In 1998 a US multinational 'announced plans to unravel the entire human genetic code by 2001', saying it intended to patent 'the most valuable gene sequences', and to sell the information to scientific institutions and drug companies. {8}

Combining this information with recent developments concerning the cloning of animals and human beings raises disturbing and even fearful prospects.

'Ownership' has been defined as 'the right to possess an item of property' and so one has to look closely at where the right comes from and how it is exercised.

Ownership rights are the property of a country's citizens and communities {9, 10}. No elected representative, government or government employee has overriding fundamental authority to hand over to multinational corporations (that is to those who own and control them {11}), or to anyone else, such ownership rights.

From
Chapter 6:
'Multinational Summits and Agreements,
Top-level Decision-making and Democracy'
Manfred Davidmann (2002)

MAI stands for 'Multilateral Agreement on Investment'. But its name does not reflect those aspects which are of deep concern. What is disturbing are not only the provisions of this proposed treaty but also that the provisions were debated in almost complete secrecy.

It appears that representatives of multinationals and governments representing the 29 richest industrialised countries, all OECD members, had been developing the MAI's provisions at the OECD (Organisation for Economic Co-operation and Development) since 1995. This seems to have been done in complete secrecy till a leaked copy became available on the Internet in 1997.

It seems that the agreement was to have been finalised in February 1998. Apparently it was adverse publicity relating to its restrictive provisions which delayed completion as concerned groups of citizens publicised their concerns. And some governments have now withdrawn their support.

> From
> Chapter 6:
> 'Multinational Summits and Agreements,
> Top-level Decision-making and Democracy'
> Manfred Davidmann (202)

Socially responsible and caring governmental legislation has to take precedence over the profit-motivated activities of corporations.

But it appears that under MAI the national governments would have handed over control, that is authority to act, over much of the economic and social welfare of their citizens to multinational corporations, that is to those who own and direct these corporations {11}, if they had agreed to this treaty.

In other words, multinationals would have been given overriding authority over democratically elected governments.

> From
> Chapter 6:
> 'Multinational Summits and Agreements,
> Top-level Decision-making and Democracy'
> Manfred Davidmann (2002)

So let us look at the kind of provisions this almost-agreed agreement on 'Multilateral Agreement on Investment' contained {9, 10}:

Democratically elected governments

- Would have had to allow multinationals access to the country.

- Would have been prevented from discriminating against foreign firms, would not be able to refuse any form of investment in any sector apart from defence.

- Would have been prevented from reducing or controlling a multinationals profits, say by minimum-wage or anti-pollution legislation, or by legislation to ensure local employment.

Multinationals would have had the right to

- Sue national governments for any profits lost through laws which discriminated against the multinational, and which harmed a multinational's interests.
- Sue national governments in an international court which would have been closed to public scrutiny.

We saw that multinationals can legally avoid paying corporation tax by transfer pricing {6} and that unitary taxation <6> {6, 33} can overcome this tax avoidance by assessing the actual profits being generated by a multinational in a particular country. Multinationals could, under MAI, have refused to be taxed by a system of unitary taxation.

As far as I know, no elected representative, government or government employee has the authority

1. to hand over to corporations (that is to those who own and control them), or to anyone else, an overriding control over the present and future, economic and social, welfare of its people, or

2. to sign away the democratic rights of their people for the self-determination of key fundamental aspects of their lives.

From
Chapter 11:
'Democracy Under Attack: Top-level Leadership
and Decision-making'
Manfred Davidmann (1998)

The Right to Know

Open Decision-taking (in Government, Enterprises, Organisations)

There should be open decision-taking at all levels of government, company, business and other organisations, commercial or otherwise.

In other words, at all levels and in all organisations.

Access to Information

All should have the right to free and unhindered access to all relevant information when requesting this.

Full information should be available to all at all levels within all organisations. This includes, for example, policy, technical, organisational, accounting or financial information, individual salaries, wages, expenses and donations.

With the exception of private or personal information about individual private citizens.

Whistle-blowing

We need to establish ways of whistle-blowing, of concerned citizens being able to inform the community of secretive decisions and of all matters which are against the public interest which are taking place within government, company, business and other organisations.

Anonymity of whistle-blowers has to be guaranteed. We need to establish ways of protecting, supporting and providing back-up for whistle-blowers.

> From
> Social Responsibility and Accountability: Summary
> Manfred Davidmann, 2002
> solhaam.org

> Also see
> 'Cooperatives and Cooperation:
> Causes of Failure, Guidelines for Success'
> Manfred Davidmann
> ISBN 978-0-85192-056-6

> and
> Social Responsibility, Profits and Social Accountability.
> Incidents, Disasters and Catastrophes.
> The Worldwide Struggle for Social Accountability.
> Community Aims and Community Leadership.
> Manfred Davidmann, 1979, 1995
> solhaam.org

The Right to Be Heard

All have the right to comment, criticise or complain in public so that they can be heard and ways have to be made available for doing so.

Within any organisation, all should have the right to write a letter on any matter affecting the organisation, or to complain in writing, signed or anonymously. Such letters or complaints should have to be published within the organisation unless publication could harm the organisation. Anonymity must be protected. All letters have to be answered honestly, sincerely, factually and openly by those concerned, regardless of their level.

Within a country or smaller communities, there has to be similar and widespread access to publicity for concerned citizens who should be fully supported by the community when wishing to comment, criticise or complain.

But one may not spread corrupting or antisocial or antidemocratic propaganda or practices.

> From
> 'Cooperatives and Cooperation:
> Causes of Failure, Guidelines for Success'
> Manfred Davidmann
> ISBN 978-0-85192-056-6
>
> The vague phrase 'Freedom of speech' is sometimes used to refer to the right to be heard. Because it is so vague, this phrase is often used to justify the spreading of corrupting and antisocial or antidemocratic propaganda and practices.
> See
> Chapter 15:
> 'Using Words to Communicate Effectively'
> Manfred Davidmann
> about 'abstractions'.

The Right to Protest and Demonstrate

While supporting and while staying within the social system and principles set out here, people need to have the right to freely associate with each other,

> for example by forming protest, support and self-help action groups,

> to peacefully protest and demonstrate to show the extent of their support and to obtain publicity, being fully supported by the community when doing so.

Public demonstrations and public protests by concerned groups are an essential survival mechanism under beginning-of-twentyfirst-century conditions.

From
Social Responsibility and Accountability: Summary
Manfred Davidmann, 2002
solhaam.org

And from
Social Responsibility, Profits and Social Accountability.
Incidents, Disasters and Catastrophes.
The Worldwide Struggle for Social Accountability.
Community Aims and Community Leadership.
Manfred Davidmann, 1979, 1995
solhaam.org

Social Costs

The social benefits and costs of any operation have to be taken into account. The gain any enterprise or organisation makes is that which accrues to the community.

But just how is the balance drawn, to what extent are social benefits and costs included in the economic analysis of alternative proposals or schemes?

Responsible leadership aims to eliminate needs so as to eliminate exploitation through needs, wants the highest possible standard of living for the people.

And since people are exploited through their needs one has to eliminate the need to struggle for survival, for mere existence.

However, there are criteria other than personal income, such as security from internal and external threats and the standards of living, housing, health service and education of the population.

And there is the question of the extent to which benefits of a benevolent social system may need to be reduced as a penalty for those who are socially irresponsible.

Purifying effluent increases costs and so reduces profits. Hence discharging unpurified effluent is more profitable to the producer but the community has to suffer the consequences. Manufacturers and suppliers tend to increase their profits by passing on to the community the social costs of their operations, costs such as disposal of packaging and waste, of redundancy and unemployment when transferring operations to countries with lower wages or fewer environmental safeguards.

However, the interests of the community have to be taken into account when taking decisions. Such social costs need to be allowed for when taking decisions, need to be charged to the enterprise or organisation which is causing them.

From
Social Responsibility and Accountability: Summary
Manfred Davidmann, 2002
solhaam.org

Social Irresponsibility

Leaderships fear bad publicity, fear public awareness of socially irresponsible behaviour and consequent impact on sales and market share, on an individual's career or on an organisation's reputation and credibility.

So an effective control of corporate and top-level irresponsibility is publicity of what is being planned or being done, making the public aware of who did or is doing what, and of who condoned or omitted to restrain, antisocial or antidemocratic activities.

Particularly so when publicity names those responsible for making antisocial decisions, and those responsible for condoning, or for omitting to restrain, antisocial activities.

From
Chapter 6:
'Multinational Summits and Agreements,
Top-level Decision-making and Democracy'
Manfred Davidmann

But how can one ensure that those in important positions become aware that they are accountable to the community and how can one make them accountable to the community?

One method may be through publicising the names of those who took the relevant decisions, who condoned the decisions and the resulting actions, who carried them out, who failed to stop them from being carried out.

There has come a point at which the interests of the community must and do take precedence over the politics of power and the interests of the owners. For this to happen, people need to act and co-operate with each other by forming pressure groups to impress the leadership with the strength of the feeling of people locally or country-wide, by getting publicity, by using the courts and by demonstrating to get the required legislation where it does not exist already, and when necessary by demonstrating to have existing legislation enforced so as to hold those accountable who fail to act for and to protect the interests of the community.

From
Social Responsibility and Accountability: Summary
Manfred Davidmann, 2002
solhaam.org

Beginnings (Origin) of Democracy

The Pentateuch's social laws and social system include a statement of fundamental and scientific social laws of behaviour, of human rights, of social and community organisation, written down about 3,400 years ago.

It is the social laws of the Pentateuch which in effect state that all are equal, that no person may exploit another or oppress so as to exploit. All have the right to be free and independent masters of their own fate and there has to be a system of social security which guarantees not just freedom from need but also protection against loss of material and spiritual independence. In effect, oppression can be and has to be resisted, struggled against and opposed.

From
Causes of Antisemitism
Manfred Davidmann, 1991, 1995
solhaam.org

Jesus Christ taught that all the laws had to be kept, that belief and practice included and had to include the Ten Commandments, the social laws and the social system of the Pentateuch. {2}

Included in the social laws of the Pentateuch, for example, are the kingship laws (Pentateuch, Deut 17: 14-20) which state that those in authority must not oppress people so as to increase their own possessions and power, that they must not put themselves above the people and so enrich themselves. They are warned against oppressing people and against forming enforcing squads or organisations so as to multiply their own power, must not be promiscuous and must not amass wealth. They must know and observe the Pentateuch law and its intent and aim to see the Pentateuch laws applied.

From
Social Concept (Policies) of the Russian Orthodox Church:
Letter to the Russians
Manfred Davidmann, 2004
solhaam.org

Chapter 18

About the Author

Manfred Davidmann is an internationally well-known and respected scientist and consultant, and author of a number of books and reports which have had considerable impact. His work usually breaks new ground and opens up new understanding and is written in meaningful and easily understood language. Outstanding is that his work is generally accepted as factual, objective and unbiased.

His works have made known and publicised the human rights, the social laws and social system, and the intense worldwide struggle to achieve them, to achieve freedom, liberty, independence and a good and secure life, here and now in this life.

Here some of his works are described under the following headings

General Management (Middle, Senior and Top Level)

Community Conflicts and Confrontations

The Worldwide Struggle for a Better Life

Brain, Mind and Group Minds. Mental Health and Corresponding Social Organisations, of Individuals, People and Communities

Government and Religion, Church and State

Cooperatives and Cooperation

General Management (Middle, Senior and Top Level)

As said already, Manfred Davidmann is an internationally well-known and respected scientist and consultant, and author of a number of books and reports which have had considerable impact. His work usually breaks new ground and opens up new understanding and is written in meaningful and easily understood language. Outstanding is that his work is generally accepted as factual, objective and unbiased.

He brings to his tasks a rare combination of practical experience, knowledge and understanding backed by years spent training middle and top-level managers. Expert knowledge is expressed in clear and meaningful language.

What Manfred Davidmann has done in his work on the general management of enterprises and communities is to lay the foundation for, and develop, what truly can be called 'management science'. He developed and defined the scope and content of General Management, in these reports:

Directing and Managing Change
Organising
Motivation

Style of Management and Leadership
Work and Pay, Incomes and Differentials: Employer, Employee
and Community

'Directing and Managing Change' (1979, 2006)
includes
adapting to change, deciding what needs to be done;
planning ahead, getting results, evaluating progress
and performance;
and appraisal interviews and target-setting meetings.

'Organising' (1981, 2006)
is a comprehensive review showing how to arrange matters so
that people can work together successfully and well. It is about
achieving effective co-operation and teamwork, particularly in
large organisations where many experts have to work together
in teams to enable aims and objectives to be achieved.

The most confused and intractable organisational problems
tend to be about functional relationships and coordinating.
Concerning these, the report's descriptions, definitions,
specifications and examples, are outstanding.

'Motivation Summary' (1982, 1998)
In 'Motivation Summary', Manfred Davidmann summarises
different motivation theories, draws on his earlier work
including evidence from his U.K. study, and utilises material
used by him for lecturing to degree-level students and for
training experienced middle and senior managers.

'Style of Management and Leadership' (1981, 2006)
Manfred Davidmann's work 'Style of Management and
Leadership' is a landmark in management and community
science and methodology. Over 770,000 copies have been
downloaded from his website, worldwide, so far (April 2011).

The term 'Participation', meaning by this 'participation in decision-making', was first coined, and defined, by Manfred Davidmann when he published his analysis and recommendations about the style of management, in 1981. His works on style of management and on participation in decision-making in management, leadership and government, are widely known, studied and applied, and sprouted a whole literature ranging from the scientific to misleading politically-motivated misrepresentations.

It was Manfred Davidmann who in 1981 formulated, clearly stated and then published ('Style of Management and Leadership', 1981) his principle that the real political struggle was not between political 'left' and 'right', but was for participation in decision-making, for the right to make the decisions.

Manfred Davidmann's concept of participative government and management, of participation in decision-making, has become a household word, in daily use when referring to government and management styles, worldwide. His concepts are applied all the way from village government and community projects to national policies and elections, are applied by cooperatives, companies and global corporations alike.

Clearly defined and described in this work is the whole scale of style of management and organising, from fully authoritarian to fully participative. It applies to community organisations, commercial enterprises, political parties, whole countries. The social assumptions underlying each of the styles are given, as are problems they create, the symptoms by which they can be recognised, and the ways people work together or against each other within them.

The extent to which authority is balanced between top and bottom, and the corresponding style of management, are also discussed. This work pulls the diverse world-wide events in labour relations and in government/people confrontation into a meaningful, clear and highly significant picture of interrelated events fitting into a consistent pattern.

Community Conflicts and Confrontations

How local and national governments are managing our affairs is of crucial importance to every citizen. Government has to make ends meet, has to bring about a rising standard of secure living, social security and an increasing quality of life for its citizens.

"There can be ups and downs but", says Manfred Davidmann, "failure to make ends meet is just as directly and surely the result of bad leadership and management as it is in any commercial enterprise." This is a severe criticism also of the kind of experts and consultants used, and of the way they are used. "The quality of one's experts and whether and how their expertise is used, and applied, are of decisive importance."

Manfred Davidmann's report 'Work and Pay, Incomes and Differentials: Employer, Employee and Community' (1981, 2007) is a concise all-embracing review and analysis of the whole subject, in clear and easily understood language. What makes this report so special is that it covers incomes and differentials from the point of view of the owner or employer, from that of the individual and his family and from that of the community, discussing their interests and requirements.

When talking about pay, incomes and differentials we are dealing with matters which are at the centre of confrontation and conflict and around which rage controversy and strife. We are dealing with matters which determine how one man stands in relation to another, with something which depends on negotiation and bargaining between those who employ and those who are employed. The result is that almost all one sees about pay and differentials is biased towards one side or the other and both points of view are then equally misleading.

But Manfred Davidmann here provides the underlying knowledge and understanding for scientific determination and prediction of rates of pay, remuneration and differentials, of remuneration scales and of national patterns of pay and differentials.

These correlations and methods represent a major breakthrough and rates of pay, incomes and differentials can be assessed with a high degree of reliability. Now pay bargaining can include agreeing basic guide-lines of the kind described here as governing pay increases.

Illustrated are National Remuneration Scales which record the remuneration pattern for a group or profession and the position of every individual in it, showing also how income depends on age and degree of success. Illustrated also is the National Remuneration Pattern which is a precise pictorial record of the differentials within a country, from top to bottom, from young to old. Both are used to assess changes in pay, remuneration and differentials for individuals, groups and professions.

However, it is easier to tell the rich to share their wealth with the poor than to persuade them to actually do so. And companies, corporations and governments, owners, managers, experts and politicians, too often work for personal gain instead of serving employees, customers or citizens, exploiting instead of serving their community.

Just consider the following examples of corporate and individual antisocial practices.

One of the most controversial operations of multinationals, transfer pricing, has been clearly described and defined by Manfred Davidmann in his report 'Multinational Operations: Transfer Pricing and Taxation' (1991, 2006).

The report showed that multinational companies were minimising their liability for corporation tax by transfer pricing, that is by making book entries which transfer profits to the country with the lowest corporation tax.

Say a multinational has increased its profits in such ways. As the government's expenses have not changed it must make up this shortfall elsewhere. From its other tax payers, say from its citizens. So its citizens pay more tax, the government can now spend the same amount as before, the multinational's profits have increased.

This tax avoidance is legal and governments have not legislated to prevent this practice.

The multinational, and this means the owners and directors of the multinational, are thus in effect taxing the country's citizens, its population, in this way increasing the multinational's profits and thus their own incomes and wealth.

A matter far removed from earning reasonable profits from providing needed quality goods and services at reasonable prices in open competition with other corporations.

Fifteen years ago, Manfred Davidmann coined the phrase 'Exporting Employment and Importing Unemployment', and pointed to, and warned about, the social and economic consequences of what is now often euphemistically called 'outsourcing' or 'globalisation'.

In his report **'Exporting and Importing of Employment and Unemployment'** (1996, 2002) he pointed out that imports were being priced at what the market will bear, or just under, and that if the enormous profit margins were left uncontrolled, these would then cause production to move from high-wage to low-wage countries. The consequence is a lowering of the standard of living in high-wage countries to that in low-wage countries, instead of a raising of the standard of living in low-wage countries to that in high wage countries.

"Unemployment has reached an unacceptable level" says Manfred Davidmann. It is a principle of economics that social costs have to be paid by those causing them. But manufacturers and suppliers tend to increase their profits by passing on to the community the social costs of their operations, costs such as disposal of packaging and waste, or of polluting.

"The social costs of unemployment have to be paid by the enterprise which caused the unemployment in the first place" says Manfred Davidmann. "Social costs need to be allowed for when making decisions, need to be charged to the enterprise or organisation which is causing them. And this applies equally well to the social costs of redundancy and unemployment when transferring operations to countries with lower wages or fewer environmental safeguards."

It was Manfred Davidmann who twenty years ago demolished the then-current economic myths about 'Price Inflation' and 'Wage Inflation', and about inflation and unemployment.

In "**Inflation, Balance of Payments and Currency Exchange Rates**" (1981, 2006), Manfred Davidmann explores how national and international accounts and accounting reflect the quality of management in national and local government, reflect multinational operations such as devaluation pricing, profits maximisation, transfer pricing, importing from low-wage countries, transferring work to low-wage countries. And he reviews different ways of balancing income and expenditure, causes of inflation, and tax avoidance.

In this report Manfred Davidmann reviews a country's ways out of a payments crisis and details the consequences of increasing interest rates, greater borrowing, selling assets or printing more money.

To give just a few examples, he:

> Shows how rising interest rates follow from balance of payments deficits.

> Shows how interest rates determine share prices and thus the extent to which pension funds are in surplus or underfunded.

> Shows how inflation affects currency exchange rates, trade and competing abroad.

Clear and meaningful language is backed by easily understood illustrations. And easy-to-follow diagrams illustrate the relationships.

The two coefficients of inequality between different countries, which Manfred Davidmann put forward in 1981 in this inflation report, are objective and effective measures of inequality and differentials.

The first he called 'Inequality between Countries'. The second, namely 'Relative Inequality between Countries', is numerically the same as the ratio between the GNP/person of the countries being compared. These measures of inequality are now in general use.

The Worldwide Struggle for a Better Life

In '**Motivation Summary**' (1982, 1998), Manfred Davidmann summarises different motivation theories, draws on his earlier work including evidence from the U.K. study, and utilises material used by him for lecturing to degree-level students and for training experienced middle and senior managers.

This chapter provides an objective, comprehensive and clear definition of 'motivation', of the factors which motivate and of what people are striving to achieve.

"Motivated behaviour is purposeful, directed towards some end" says Manfred Davidmann. "The driving force is need. The direction is towards perceived reward and away from perceived punishment."

And in the workplace one aims to achieve either job satisfaction or money rewards or both. "Motivation towards better performance depends on the satisfaction of needs for responsibility, achievement, recognition and growth."

One works to achieve that which one needs and which one does not have. "Attaining goals leads to feelings of self-respect, strength and confidence", and "persistent lack of rewards leads to a view of society as being hostile and unrewarding".

Manfred Davidmann's fundamental work on motivation, '**The Will to Work: What People Struggle to Achieve**' (1981, 2006), includes a detailed step-by-step listing of what people are struggling to achieve, their needs and wants, their achievements and objectives. It is a unique analysis of the worldwide struggle for a better life at all levels of life and development, in all countries.

What we see in the working environment is each person, family or community struggling to advance at their own level of development.

Manfred Davidmann here clearly defines and describes motivation, its basis and 'motivating'.

Starting by considering motivation from the point of view of the employer (productivity, remuneration, job satisfaction), this leads to considering what people want and what they struggle to achieve.

A key part of this chapter is community orientated, including a detailed step-by-step listing of what people are struggling to achieve, their needs and wants, their achievements and objectives.

It is a unique analysis of the worldwide struggle for a better life at all levels of life and development, in all countries. What we see in the working environment is each person, family or community struggling to advance at their own level of development.

This progression shows underdeveloped and developed people as they are, human beings at different stages of an identical struggle for a better life against those who wish to profit from their condition.

And you can assess how far the country/community you are living in has advanced in this struggle for independence and a good life for all, or where you are yourself on this scale.

Highlights are Figure 1 (Motivation of Directors) and Figure 3 (People's Needs and Wants, Achievements and Objectives: The Struggle for Independence and a Good Life).

In **"Family, Sex and the Individual"** (1998, 2011), Manfred Davidmann exposes the causes of what seems to be a progressive breaking down of family life and of social strength.

Clearly described and defined is the role of the family under modern conditions, and the differences between the behaviour of human beings and that of the primitive animals from which human beings evolved. He illustrated the underlying basis of teamwork within the family, stating the various roles and responsibilities and functional relationships of its members for effective teamwork within the family.

He was the first to clearly describe and show, thirteen years ago, the effects of increasing life spans on the family, on its members and on their responsibilities.

We now live much longer and the time spent full-time at home looking after the family places women at a disadvantage when returning to work outside the family after the children have been brought up. So women need to be supported when returning to work.

And Manfred Davidmann showed that the family compensates women for the life-long effects of their contribution towards the upbringing of the children. It is the role of the spouse, of the husband, to continue to provide for the family. A life-long contribution from him which means she does not lose out for the rest of her life because she stayed at home to look after the children, the husband's input into the family balancing her input of bringing up the children and looking after the family's members.

This work also investigates the impact of casual sexual relations and its effects on individuals, family and community, on the social strength of individuals and communities.

And it examines and relates dominance and confrontation within the family to that in the working environment and considers oppression and exploitation within and outside the family.

Human rights are based on controlling primitive dominating behaviour, on concern, care and affection for our young and our families, for people and for our communities. Human rights express themselves in co-operation and teamwork between men and women to achieve a good life of high quality.

It is in democracies that a high standard of living has been achieved. In democracies people can struggle openly for a better life but we see that what has been gained has to be defended and extended.

This work is an unprecedented and comprehensive overview, states new insights, proves basic underlying causes.

The main report **What People are Struggling Against: How Society is Organised for Controlling and Exploiting People** (1998, 2002), brings together key conclusions from four studies undertaken by Manfred Davidmann to obtain a better understanding of why people have to struggle throughout their adult lives, in all countries and organisations, at all levels, to maintain and improve their standard of living and quality of life. We know what people are struggling to achieve and so this study was undertaken to explore why people have to struggle by looking at what they are struggling against.

This work looks at the way 'Economics' is being used to misinform and mislead the general public, and looks at the role and vested interests of experts. It describes how companies (corporations) accumulate their capital and reserves from moneys taken from customers and how people's massive savings are placed under the control of others. And shows how taxpayers' moneys are used in different ways to enlarge the profits of companies.

It discusses and illustrates the internal struggles taking place in political parties and all other organisations, for achieving greater democracy and against those wishing to overpower democratic processes of decision-making.

In **'Democracy, Socialism and Communism: The Worldwide Struggle for a Better Life'** (2008) Manfred Davidmann outlined the battlefield in these terms:

Participative (democratic) organisation rests on the population electing representatives, on the basis of each person having one vote. Representatives are responsible to, and accountable to, the population for putting into effect policies decided by the population.

What underlies participative organisation (democracy) is decision-making by the people at the level of the people.

What needs to be stressed is that in a participative (democratic) organisation policies are decided by a well-informed population at the level of the population and that policies then become binding on management or government. It was Manfred Davidmann who formulated, clearly stated and then published ('Style of Management and Leadership', 1981) his principle that the real political struggle was not between political 'left' and 'right', but was for participation in decision-making, for the right to make the decisions.

Representatives, governments or government officials do not have the authority or right to reduce or sign away the participative (democratic) rights of the electors, of the population.

The real struggle is not between political left and right, but is a struggle for participation, that is for the right of the population to be well-informed and to make the decisions which then become binding on management or government, as outlined by Manfred Davidmann in 'Multinational Summits and Agreements, Top-level Decision-making and Democracy' (2002).

Brain, Mind and Group Minds. Mental Health and Corresponding Social Organisations, of Individuals, People and Communities.

In 'How the Human Brain Developed and How the Human Mind Works' (1998, 2006), Manfred Davidmann explains how the human brain evolved and functions, how the human mind works, and how brain and mind interact. This fundamental work provides fascinating insights clearly expressed in meaningful language, including a much clearer appreciation of the different functions of the two halves of the brain, and of the different kinds of sleep and memory.

The work showed how brain and mind determine what people do and how they do it, what people aim to achieve and how in the struggle for a better life we adapt to the world in which we live.

It proved that images penetrate deeply into the ancient and primitive parts of the human brain and how certain images can be "brutalising society, seemingly legalising, making acceptable, inconsiderate and unfeeling behaviour towards other people."

Relating the functioning of the brain to behavior, this report showed how human behavior is affected by the primitive instincts of our reptilian ancestors. It seems that instinctive behavior has to be controlled, and is modified according to the environment in which we find ourselves, in every generation, and that the mammalian and human parts of the brain play a major part in this.

Manfred Davidmann considers that humane behavior is based on feelings of care and affection for the young and for the family, and then for other people and the community. From this emerges a sense of social responsibility: People matter and are important, and need to be treated well.

A key finding of Manfred Davidmann's report is that the right hemisphere of the human brain is able to communicate by using images with the brain's older and more primitive component organs which have no verbal skills. And this enables us to communicate intentionally (that is "consciously") with our autonomic nervous system and by visualizing control of body functions and to affect our body's immune system. Clinical trials have shown remarkable success in areas such as the treatment of cancer and heart disease.

The day-night-day sleep pattern, the "DEEP sleep"/"REM sleep" sequence, and how the different halves of the brain communicate by means of images with the older parts of the brain, are correlated and illustrated. Manfred Davidmann makes the point that the brain paralyzes the body to enable dreaming to take place, that dreaming performs an essential function, and he explains the role and meaning of dreams and dreaming.

Manfred Davidmann considers that humane behavior is based on feelings of care and affection for the young and for the family, and then for other people and the community. From this emerges a sense of social responsibility: People matter and are important, and need to be treated well.

As a result of the work in this report, there emerged a much clearer appreciation of what happens during the course of a night's sleep, and clear explanations of the role of dreaming and the meaning of dreams.

The report explores the functioning and role of the two halves of the human brain and the relationship between them. It is the right half which usually communicates with the primitive parts of the human brain and this is related to the functioning of the autonomic nervous system and the immune system.

When Manfred Davidmann first announced his Group Mind Theory in 1973, this theory and his concepts and terms such as 'group minds', were completely new and unheard of. The second edition was published in 1998 and made available on the internet in 1999.

His "human group minds and how they function", that is the Group Mind Science he originated, are now widely quoted and discussed, have sprouted a whole literature about group minds ranging from publications of scientific institutions and in reference books, to unscientific misleading look-alikes about human minds.

In 'The Human Group Mind and How It Works' (1973, 1978), Manfred Davidmann outlines, describes, uncovers and proves the subconscious existence and workings of group minds by the extraordinary way in which they affect and determine what individuals and communities do. This is shown to explain how human communities and society are organised and function, countrywide and worldwide, and consequent confrontations and struggles from dictatorship to democracy. We are here looking at what motivates and drives human beings, seeing how the mind shapes the way in which we live, suffer, struggle and achieve.

Included are comprehensive but concise reviews of mental health and mental illness. There are sections which discuss how conflict arises within the mind, and the mind theories of Freud and of Jung are reviewed.

Manfred Davidmann's Group Mind Science is proved by the way in which it explains and predicts not only the mental problems of individuals but also society's social problems.

It predicts and explains the way in which society is organised as well as human activities and organisation, explains dominance, co-operation, non-conformity and conflict as well as why people are struggling and what they are struggling against.

The subconscious existence and workings of group minds become apparent by the extraordinary way in which they affect and determine what individuals and communities do. The chapters of this book which deal with how we live and struggle, with the way our communities and societies are organised and function, describe how our minds shape our lives, communities and society, and uncover the workings of group minds.

Manfred Davidmann's Group Mind Science represents substantial beneficial healing powers. Following the work of Freud and Jung, it is regarded as scientifically proved, as meaningful, objective and practical, as applying worldwide to all human beings in all societies and cultures and at all stages of development.

Manfred Davidmann's Group Mind Science is based on deep knowledge and understanding of the real world, and proved by the way in which it explains and predicts human activities and organisation as well as the mental problems of individuals and society's social problems. Its insights enable us to solve such problems effectively.

The work about 'The Human Group Mind', on how human minds work and operate, on human group minds, consists of four consecutive parts, as follows:

'The Human Group Mind and How It Works' (1973, 1998)
>   The 'Group Mind' science is outlined and described. There are sections which discuss how conflict arises within the mind,

mental health and illness, dominance, creativity and hearing voices.

Shows how our minds shape our lives, communities and society.

'Manipulated Communities and Populations' (1973, 1998)

The workings of group minds is shown to explain how human communities and society are organised and the consequent confrontations and struggles from dictatorship to democracy.

Discusses how mass media are forming and manipulating public opinions and illustrates how writers and artists have been sensing and expressing the underlying subconscious reality.

'Manipulated Individuals' (1973, 1998)

Shows how emotional unreasoning behaviour is being reinforced to make it easier to mislead and exploit.

Reviews available information on incidence and causes of psychosomatic illnesses.

'Freedom, Liberty and Good Life: Overcoming Corrupt Manipulations' (1973, 2001)

The Group Mind science of the way in which human minds work is proved by the way in which it explains and predicts human activities and organisation as well as mental problems of individuals and society's social problems. Its insights enable us to solve such problems effectively.

When individuals, communities and populations are manipulated, then behaviour is all-important. This report shows how we can overcome corrupt manipulations, how behaviour determines our standard of living and the quality of our lives, and describes the kind of behaviour and social organisation on which depend liberty, freedom and a good and secure life for all.

Government and Religion, Church and State

Manfred Davidmann's The God-given Human Rights, Social Laws and Social System (2003) is a comprehensive statement of the God-given human rights and obligations which underlie freedom, liberty, independence and well-being. They underlie and determine a good life of high quality. People at all stages of development are struggling to achieve these rights and benefits, all over the planet.

253

Directly relevant to today's social and economic problems, these rights and obligations determine the quality of life in areas such as social and economic security, social responsibility and accountability, ownership and decision-making, government and management, humane behaviour, teamwork and trustful cooperation.

> These human rights, these social rules and this social system, are the very foundation of the three main religions of Judaism, Christianity and Islam.

> Manfred Davidmann discovered that what these religions have in common is that in each case a ruling elite succeeded in bypassing or overturning the religion's essential God-given benevolent social provisions and human rights, in this way exposing their communities and whole populations to oppression and exploitation.

What Manfred Davidmann has done with his works on the Pentateuch and the Bible, on religion and church-state relations, is to expose and correct the misinterpretations and mistranslations of the past. His works are major breakthroughs, constituting essential information for understanding the meaning and significance of the Pentateuch and the Bible.

The Pentateuch records and details the Social Cause-and-Effect Relationship, a fundamental scientific law which is stated as such and which was discovered by Manfred Davidmann. In his 'Struggle for Freedom: The Social Cause-and-Effect Relationship' (1978, 2002) he shows that this law states that the consequences of keeping or not keeping the social laws are inescapable, that what happens to one is in the end the inevitable result of one's own behavior. It is stated to enable people to benefit from knowing the effects of their behaviour.

Ignorance of these rules of behavior is no excuse and the relationship applies to all. History and social science confirm it, the prophets knew and understood it and predicted accordingly. Jesus confirmed it; the Koran records Prophet Mohammed repeatedly confirming the Pentateuch, referring to it both as a guide and as a warning.

Whole communities prosper or suffer as a consequence of their collective behavior. Manfred Davidmann says, "The consequences of our behavior cannot be avoided but we can change the course of events by changing our behavior."

He states "A new factor has entered the equation. It is now possible for the first time in the history of human beings on this planet for just one or only a few socially irresponsible persons to do something or to introduce changes which could destroy us all or else make this planet uninhabitable for human beings."

The Ten Commandments are so important and are so well known because it is behaviour in accordance with these laws which is the basis for people trusting each other and so for people co-operating and working well with each other. They are listed in 'Struggle for Freedom: The Social Cause-and-Effect Relationship' (1978, 2002) both in biblical language and in plain English.

It is the Ten Commandments as a whole which underlie freedom, independence and strength to oppose and resist oppression. Wherever there is any spiritual and material freedom today it exists because people followed these laws (rules) of behaviour and it exists to the extent to which they do so. In other words, following the provisions of the law results in freedom and ensures it, ensures strength and security.

History shows that in the past the people have been betrayed again and again, by non-observant leaderships no matter whether right or left and by so-called orthodox or fundamentalist leaderships who weakened the application of the law so as to be able to oppress the people in order to exploit them. It was those who did not follow the law who in the past grasped power and then weakened and defeated the hope for achieving freedom and a good life for the people and thus in due course for all humanity.

It is equally certain that the same battle is being fought today and it is just as certain that on the one hand is the opportunity to gain freedom while on the other hand our defeat can only result in mankind rapidly destroying itself.

To free ourselves from mental conditioning and brainwashing we have to follow the Ten Commandments and apply the social laws and the social system of the Pentateuch.

In 'Democracy, Socialism and Communism: The Worldwide Struggle for a Better Life' (2008), Manfred Davidmann exposes what people are struggling against, the secretive manipulations of bureaucracy, oppressors and exploiters.

He shows that underlying Judaism, Christianity and Islam are the same fundamental benevolent and egalitarian social laws and social system which also underlie Democracy, Socialism and Communism (See 'The God-given Human Rights, Social Laws and Social System' (2003) above). He traces them to their origin and proves from contemporary written records that in each case the ruling and religious hierarchies (bureaucracies) soon bypassed or annulled the 'God-given' social laws and social system, replacing them with 'man-made', ruler- and hierarchy-serving obedience-demanding protest-silencing indoctrination.

It is these revisionist versions which are being taught and believed today and here we see clearly the causes of present controversies and conflicts between church and state, between beliefs and practice, in these religions.

This work also covers dominance and confrontation within the family and in the working environment, how men and women relate to each other, and the role of the family. The family is decisive in determining the quality of life; it is a source of strength and support in a time of need.

It shows how the media are being used for 'social engineering', a kind of brainwashing aimed at turning the struggle of the working population into 'self-defeating' directions, into 'scoring own goals'.

Manfred Davidmann's groundbreaking discoveries about Judaism, Christianity and Islam, published over twenty-five years, are acknowledged as major advances. And in his report "**Judaism, Christianity and Islam**" (2004), we see for the first time the complete sequence of consecutive events.

Manfred Davidmann has shown that underlying Judaism, Christianity and Islam are the Pentateuch's benevolent and egalitarian social laws and social system which include laws protecting the people by restraining the behaviour of their rulers. Those in positions of trust, responsibility or authority must not oppress people and the laws forbid personal gain from the misuse of wealth or position.

He not only proves the meaning and intent of Genesis, the first volume of the Pentateuch, but also exposes the mistranslations and political misrepresentations of the past. For example he established the meaning of the names of God which had been 'lost'.

Manfred Davidmann's work '**The Meaning of Genesis: Creation, Evolution and the Origin of Evil**' (2000) proves that there is no conflict or contradiction between Darwin's theory of evolution by natural selection and what is written in Genesis. Conflicts have arisen because some parts of Genesis have been mistranslated or misinterpreted.

The 'Creationism' hypothesis apparently assumes that the resulting erroneous text correctly states God's deeds. Following the publication of Manfred Davidmann's work, and of the publicity it generated, the 'Creationism' hypothesis was abandoned as untenable. But a similar hypothesis was then put forward called 'Intelligent Design' which apparently assumes that the same erroneous text could correctly state the deeds of some other supernatural being.

256

What Manfred Davidmann proves in **'The Meaning of Genesis: Creation, Evolution and the Origin of Evil'** (2000) is that Genesis clearly states the evolution from reptilian to mammalian instincts, feelings and behaviour and the evolution and behaviour of human beings from humanoids (animals resembling humans) through Homo erectus (early man) to Homo sapiens (human beings, ourselves).

For example, the allegory telling about Adam and Eve in the Garden of Eden describes the evolution of Homo sapiens (human beings, ourselves) from Homo erectus. Genesis records that childbirth became more difficult as a result of the increased brain size (evolution of neocortex) which enabled Homo sapiens to know the difference between good and evil and to choose between them. Also stated is the necessary division of work between the male and the female, as equals in different roles, in protecting and bringing up their children, and much more.

What Manfred Davidmann has done with his works on the Pentateuch and the Bible, on religion and church-state relations, is to expose and correct the misinterpretations and mistranslations of the past. His works are major breakthroughs, constituting essential information for understanding the meaning and significance of the Pentateuch and the Bible.

For example, in "**Meaning and Significance of the Names of God in Genesis**" (2000), Manfred Davidmann proved the meaning and significance of the different names of God which had been lost.

In "**Meaning and Intent of Genesis: Essential Notes on Hebrew Grammar,**" (2000) he stated the fundamental rules which were ignored at time of translation because required background knowledge was not available, with consequent mistranslations.

And in "**Bible Translations, Versions, Codes and Hidden Information in Bible and Talmud**" (2001), he showed how changes made in the past obscured the intended meaning.

In his book **'ISLAM: Basis - Past - Present - Future'**, (2003, 2010) Manfred Davidmann assembles, evaluates and objectively records the events of the formative years which shaped Islam. He enables one to understand how Islam came to be and its present beliefs and practices, conflicts and confrontations.

Knowing about Prophet Mohammed's struggle for recognition of his mission and message, is of vital importance if one wishes to understand what Mohammed taught and the Koran. Just what upset the elite so thoroughly and persistently that it caused him and his followers to be harshly opposed and actively persecuted?

The events and struggles which took place after Mohammed's death, and how the Koran and Islam came to be, shaped Muslim belief and practice, formed Sunnism and Shiism, underlie today's conflicts and confrontations within Islam.

Cooperatives and Cooperation

When people are exploited and oppressed they co-operate with each other to escape from poverty, to overcome exploitation and oppression. As do people wishing to improve working conditions and the quality of their lives. They get together and form co-operatives.

Manfred Davidmann's book **'Co-operatives and Co-operation: Causes of Failure, Guidelines for Success'** (1973-2006, 2011) is based on and includes a series of eight studies of co-operatives and mutual societies which were undertaken to determine causes of failure and reasons for success, to see how these enterprises were controlled and managed, to learn from their mistakes, to understand why members of established co-ops are dissatisfied with what they are getting from their co-ops.

As a matter of principle, all profits (surplus) made by a co-operative or mutual society belongs to its members as individuals. Any profit which is retained and added to reserves is the total of amounts which in effect were deducted from the profit share of each individual member.

Manfred Davidmann showed with these case studies that, for example, co-ops and mutual societies retain much of the profits and that their members then cease to be entitled to them.

Component Case Studies

Mutual Societies
Trustee Savings Bank
Credit Unions
Building Societies

Consumer Co-ops
Co-operative Retail Services Ltd
Co-operative Wholesale Society Ltd
The Co-operative Bank PLC
Co-operative Insurance Society Ltd

Producer (Worker) Co-ops
John Lewis Partnership plc
Mondragon Co-operatives
Kibbutzim (Plural of 'kibbutz')

Role of Managers under Different Styles of Management (1982, 1998) is a short summary of the role of managers under authoritarian and participative styles of management. It also covers decision making and the basic characteristics of each style.

And **Using Words to Communicate Effectively,** shows how to communicate more effectively, covering aspects of thinking, writing, speaking and listening as well as formal and informal communications. Consists of guidelines found useful by university students and practising middle and senior managers.

Manfred Davidmann

ISLAM: Basis – Past – Present- Future

Knowing about Prophet Mohammed's struggle for recognition of his mission and message, is of vital importance if one wishes to understand what Mohammed taught and the Koran. Just what upset the elite so thoroughly and persistently that it caused him and his followers to be harshly opposed and actively persecuted?

The events and struggles which took place after Mohammed's death, and how the Koran and Islam came to be, shaped Muslim belief and practice, formed Sunnism and Shiism, underlie today's conflicts and confrontations within Islam.

In this book Manfred Davidmann assembles, evaluates and objectively records the events of the formative years which shaped Islam. He enables one to understand how Islam came to be and its present beliefs and practices, conflicts and confrontations. Comprehensiveness of information, and depth of analysis, can be judged by the book's chapter headings:

Prophet Mohammed's Struggle for a Better Life for All

Text, Language, Dialect and Interpretation of the Koran

The Divine Right to Rule

Compiling the Koran: Hadiths (Traditions) State the Underlying Reality

Caliph Uthman's Rearrangement of the 'as revealed' Koran's Chapters

Prophet Mohammed's Word of Allah and the Voice of the Ruling Elite

Muslims and Jews

Church and State, Government and Religion

    Judaism, Christianity and Islam

    Religion, Government and Education

The book, and the earlier individual research reports which are included in it, contains not only Manfred Davidmann's clear and factual compilations about what actually happened after Mohammed's death, but also his comprehensive and detailed findings, definitions and conclusions about the '**Text, Language, Dialect and Interpretation of the Koran**' (2003), about how the Koran was compiled and about its contents. Published 2003, guided to some extent by some of the Koran's 'abbreviated letters'.

Manfred Davidmann

God and People:
The Social Laws and Social System Underlying
Judaism, Christianity, Islam and Democracy

This book is a collection of works by Manfred Davidmann about the God-given human rights, social laws and social system, and about the worldwide struggle to achieve them, to achieve freedom, liberty, independence and a good and secure life, here and now in this life.

Manfred Davidmann not only proves the meaning and intent of Genesis, the first volume of the Pentateuch, but also exposes the mistranslations and political misrepresentations of the past. For example he establishes the meaning of the names of God which 'had been lost'.

Clearly described and defined is the role of the family under modern conditions, and the differences between the behaviour of human beings and that of the primitive animals from which human beings evolved.

The main chapter headings are:

> The Real World in which We Live
>
> The God-given Human Rights, Social Laws and Social System
>
> Struggle for Freedom, Liberty and Independence: The Social Cause-and-Effect Relationship
>
> Family and Community: Family, Sex and the Individual
>
> The Meaning of Genesis

Manfred Davidmann is an internationally well-known and respected scientist and consultant, and author of a number of books and reports which have had considerable impact. His work usually breaks new ground and opens up new understanding and is written in meaningful and easily understood language. Outstanding is that his work is generally accepted as factual, objective and unbiased.

Manfred Davidmann

THE HUMAN MIND AND HOW IT WORKS:
Group Minds in Action: How the Human Group Mind Shapes the Quality of Our Life and Living

Manfred Davidmann shows how the human brain evolved and functions, how the human mind works, and how brain and mind interact. This fundamental work provides fascinating insights clearly expressed in meaningful language, shows how brain and mind determine what people do and how they do it, what people aim to achieve and how in the struggle for a better life we adapt to the world in which we live.

The chapters of this book which deal with how our communities and societies are organised and function, describe how our group minds shape our lives, communities and society, explain the consequent confrontations and struggles from dictatorship to democracy.

Relating the functioning of the brain to behaviour, this work shows how human behavior is affected by the primitive instincts of our reptilian ancestors. There are sections which discuss how conflict arises within the mind, mental health and illness, dominance, creativity and hearing voices.

Comprehensiveness of information, and depth of analysis, can be judged by the book's chapter headings:

> The Human Brain and the Human Mind
> > How the Human Brain Developed and How the Human Mind Works
>
> The Human Group Mind
> > The Human Group Mind and How It Works
> > Manipulated Communities and Populations
> > Manipulated Individuals
> > Freedom, Liberty and Good Life: Overcoming Corrupt Manipulations
>
> What People Struggle to Achieve
> > Motivation Summary
> > What People are Struggling Against: How Society is Organised for Controlling and Exploiting People
> > The Will to Work: What People Struggle to Achieve
>
> Worldwide Struggle
> > Democracy, Socialism and Communism: The Worldwide Struggle for a Better Life

Manfred Davidmann

Cooperatives and Cooperation:
Causes of Failure, Guidelines for Success

When people are exploited and oppressed they cooperate with each other to escape from poverty, to overcome exploitation and oppression. As do people wishing to improve working conditions and the quality of their lives. They get together and form cooperatives.

Different forms of cooperatives tackle different kinds of problems. What they have in common is that they serve their members and the community, aiming to improve the quality of life for their members.

As a matter of principle, all profit (surplus) made by a cooperative or mutual society belongs to its members as individuals. Any profit which is retained and added to reserves is the total of amounts which in effect were deducted from the profit share of each individual member.

This book is based on a series of eight studies of cooperatives and mutual societies which were undertaken to determine causes of failure and reasons for success, to see how these enterprises were controlled and managed, to learn from their mistakes.

Its conclusions and recommendations are relevant and cover fundamental and practical problems of coops and mutual societies, of members, of direction, management and control.

Manfred Davidmann showed with these case studies that, for example, coops and mutual societies retain much of the profits and that their members then cease to be entitled to them.

Component Case Studies

Mutual Societies
Trustee Savings Bank
Credit Unions
Building Societies

Consumer Coops
Cooperative Retail Services Ltd
Cooperative Wholesale Society Ltd
The Cooperative Bank PLC
Cooperative Insurance Society Ltd

Producer (Worker) Coops
John Lewis Partnership plc
Mondragon Cooperatives
Kibbutzim (Plural of 'kibbutz')

Manfred Davidmann

Management and Leadership:
Local, National, Multinational (Global),
Principles and Practice

The term 'Participation', meaning by this 'participation in decision-making', was first coined, and defined, by Manfred Davidmann when he published his analysis and recommendations about the style of management. His works on style of management and on participation in decision-making in management, leadership and government, are widely known, studied and applied.

Manfred Davidmann brings to his tasks a rare combination of practical experience, knowledge and understanding backed by years spent training middle and top-level managers. Expert knowledge is expressed in clear and meaningful language and easy-to-follow diagrams illustrate the relationships.

The main chapter headings are:

Style of Management and Leadership

Motivation

Directing and Managing Change

Organising

Work and Pay

Inflation, Balance of Payments and Currency Exchange Rates

Using Words to Communicate Effectively

How local and national governments are managing our affairs is of crucial importance to every citizen. Government has to make ends meet, has to bring about a rising standard of secure living, social security and an increasing quality of life for its citizens.

"There can be ups and downs but", says Manfred Davidmann, "failure to make ends meet is just as directly and surely the result of bad leadership and management as it is in any commercial enterprise."

Manfred Davidmann reviews ways of balancing income and expenditure, causes of inflation, and tax avoidance, reviews ways out of a payments crisis and details the consequences of increasing interest rates, greater borrowing, selling assets or printing more money.

One works to achieve that which one needs and which one does not have. "Attaining goals leads to feelings of self-respect, strength and confidence", and "persistent lack of rewards leads to a view of society as being hostile and unrewarding".